THE CHRISTIAN ENCOUNTERS

Town and Country
AMERICA

GILES C. EKOLA

CONCORDIA
PUBLISHING
HOUSE

ST. LOUIS

LONDON

TO MY PARENTS

Concordia Publishing House, St. Louis, Missouri
Concordia Publishing House Ltd., London, E. C. 1
© 1967 Concordia Publishing House
Library of Congress Catalog Card No. 67-29790
MANUFACTURED IN THE UNITED STATES OF AMERICA

CONTENTS

PREFACE

Life in town and country, nonmetropolitan areas, is taking on a new shape because of national and world developments.

Land and space are under the pressure of increased demand. For example, every mile of modern highway wipes out the equivalent of a 50-acre park.

Agriculture on the world scene is falling behind the population explosion. Gunnar Myrdal, speaking at the 1966 World Land Reform Conference in Rome, said: "A future historian may place the beginning of the hunger crisis at a point in time already past."

Pollution of land, water, and air by industry, agriculture, and community is compelling social and physical scientists and other citizens to rethink our resource-use policies and exploitative practices.

Town and country resources are essential to the people in cities, suburbs, and countryside alike. Town and country problems cannot be met, nor potentials fully realized, by town and country people alone. Also urban problems and potentials, we have come to learn, are larger than the urban situation itself. Confronted by the nature and scope of society today, people of metropolitan and nonmetropolitan areas need to become reasonably informed about economic and social issues in both settings.

A search for wholeness is under way by political leaders, social scientists, and churchmen. It is sometimes thought that identifying the parts of society and giving special attention to them may jeopardize wholeness. Yet when a part is not identified nor given special attention, that part becomes obscure and is less able to perform its functions. Whenever this happens, wholeness already is fading.

It is a contention here that town and country has come to lack identification, has dropped too far from view, has too few spokesmen. Our purpose is to identify some common interests and issues of town and country and urban areas and to bring them into constructive relation.

The relationship between the metropolitan and the nonmetropolitan populations of the American society may be compared to that between the infield and the outfield of a baseball team. Each is manned and played somewhat differently, requiring different specialties. Each understands and works with the other. Both function in the interest of the whole. Both play the same ball and have the same overall objective.

6

I acknowledge the influence and counsel of E. W. Mueller while I was a seminarian, parish pastor, and his fellow staff member. His national leadership of church in town and country began in 1945, when he became a staff member of the National Lutheran Council. He is an insight-sharing mentor of hundreds of pastors. It is a privilege to have been his associate for five and a half years. To know him is to grow.

GILES C. EKOLA

1 Town and Country in Balance

New Jersey is one of our most urbanized states. Yet a recent decision by its citizens affirms the place and importance of town and country in contemporary America.

A few years ago farms were being sold to housing developers and industries at an alarming rate. The question farmers faced was not whether they were going to sell for urban development but when. Behind the trend lay the issue of taxation. Farmland was being taxed at a rate three times that of any other state. Economic pressures were rapidly reducing New Jersey's agriculture.

Farmers, educators, businessmen, industrial leaders, people in the professions, and others became alarmed and mounted a campaign to bring the issue before the public. What kind of state do we want? One without farms and open space, entirely of cities, concrete, and urban sprawl? So successful was the campaign that when the legislature in 1963 submitted the issue to a popular referendum the vote was 3 to 1 to change the tax policy so that farms are now taxed on the basis of agricultural and not on speculative land value.[1]

Circumstances and issues vary from state to state and region to region, but the experience of New Jersey points to a new view of agriculture, open space, and small towns. The interwoven relationships between large cities and town and country areas, between metropolitan and nonmetropolitan counties, are being discovered to be the warp and woof of one and the same fabric.

Titles Identify Common Stake in Town and Country

Urban citizens need to become familiar with issues and potentials in town and country areas. Harvey Cox says, "Urban-secular man is pragmatic." He implies a highly informed pragmatism. If this is correct (and there is every reason to agree), then it is the urban person who has a reasoned interest in town and country.

Social and physical scientists have the institutions, population, and natural resources of nonmetropolitan counties under constant study. A few recent titles suggest something of the interest there is in what goes on outside the urban orbit: *A Place to Live, A Wilderness Bill of Rights, Agriculture and the Public Interest, City Man's Guide to the Farm Problem, Earth: The Stuff of Life, Land and Water for Recreation, Outdoor Recreation for America, Restoring the Quality of Our Environment, The Quiet Crisis,* and *Water.*

Farmers, ranchers, and agriculture services in rural America have demonstrated their capacities for entrepreneurship and productivity. In other countries the capacity for entrepreneurship is either not yet widely developed or is denied for economic, political, and/or technological reasons. Further, the resources of climate, land area, soil, and water may not permit a highly diversified and productive agriculture.

Entrepreneurship and productivity imply the acquisition and utilization of information that is wide ranging and has long-term goals. Again, a few recent titles may suggest something of the concerns town and country people have in their own circumstance: *Agricultural Bargaining Power, American Farm Policy, Farms and Farmers in an Urban Age, Handbook of Agricultural Occupations, Huelga, Individual Freedom and the Economic Organization of Agriculture, Land Use Problems and Policy in the United States, Leadership in a Small Town, Reapportionment: The Law and Politics of Equal Representation,* and *Rural Recreation for Profit.*

Town and Country as a Term

Town and country is a term that has been around for a long while. Definitions vary, depending on when it is used and who is using it. The term itself is not sociologically definitive. Rather it describes the countryside — open country, villages, towns, and small cities. A background sketch of its usage may be helpful.

"Town and country" is used in England, Canada, and the United States. Similar terms may be used in other countries. In 1932 the British government employed it to describe a national planning act to prepare "urban, potentially urban, or distinctively rural" areas for the future.[2]

In the United States and Canada the term is used chiefly by various denominations in preference to "rural."

The latter term, although often used loosely, appears to have lost much of its validity as an adequate antonym to "urban." Probably "rural" became obsolete sometime during or after World War II. Something more descriptive of the emerging relationships of open country and various-size communities was needed. "Town and country" came to be used by the churches. It describes a demographic area for mission, from open country to communities up to populations of 5, 10, or 25 thousand (depending on the denomination using it).

The U. S. Department of Agriculture has used the term for many years and continues to use it, particularly in its relations with the respective denominations.

The National Lutheran Council employed the phrase "church in town and country" from 1958 to 1966 to mean a demographic and geographic area of mission responsibility from open country to communities up to 25,000. In practical or nonscientific use in recent years town and country is regarded by many as being synonymous with nonmetropolitan counties (or, in general, counties with communities not in excess of 50,000 population and not adjoining a Standard Metropolitan Area). In literature dealing with populations or counties outside metropolitan areas, the terms nonmetropolitan or nonmetropolitan counties occur frequently.

We use the term town and country because it is positive, implies more than rural although rural is included, and conveys an image of the North American countryside together with its villages, towns, and small cities. Further, we use the terms rural America, the American countryside, and nonmetropolitan areas interchangeably with town and country.

The use of terms is continually open to discussion and to personal preference. The intention here is to clarify present usage, not to force a term on anyone.

Nevertheless, until replaced in both technical and popular vocabularies a term is very much alive.

What Town and Country Involves

Town and country covers the landmass and the bulk of our natural resources. Over 90 percent of the land area in the U.S. is countryside, nonmetropolitan.

A comparison of the number of counties in both settings presents another facet of the scope of town and country. Of the 3,150 counties in the United States, 350 are in the 212 (plus) Standard Metropolitan Statistical Areas. The remaining 2,800 counties constitute what we call town and country.

At a time of unprecedented competition for space, town and country offers room essential for growth. Wise land use, based on the capabilities of the soils, is one of the critical issues of our encounter with town and country America.

What about the population? Growth in the numbers of people living in town and country may not be readily visible when articles, publications, and speakers frequently report a declining "rural" population. These reports are most frequently made on the base of one or two decades. When the population of town and country is compared over a span of five or six decades, a different picture comes into view. Today the population is around 65 to 70 million; in 1900 it was around 45 million. Growth is taking place although it is not as pronounced as in metropolitan areas. Many forecasters predict that by 1980 about 80 percent of the nation's people will live in metropolitan areas, and they may be right; but such developments as the increase of rural nonfarm residents, dispersal of small and large industries, development of new towns just beyond metropolitan counties, expansion of food processing in rural areas, rural community development, and other factors may tamper with their figures.

The world's first-ranking agricultural establishment in breadth, diversity, and productivity is situated in town and country, U. S. A. As people fly over our countryside and study the landscape from a bird's-eye view, the thousands of farms, orchards, and ranches—the millions of cultivated acres—impress on the mind something of the diversity and magnitude of American agriculture.

The labor and management of farms, orchards, and ranches is supplied by the largest grouping of self-employed people in the U. S. They are also the largest single group of consumers and users of credit. Equipped with highly developed mechanization, various technologies, and scientific management, our agriculture and agribusiness constitute a phenomenon unmatched in history.

Forested areas occupy some 760 million acres, or about one third of the U. S. total of 2.3 billion acres. Some 510 million acres are suitable for pulp, sawlogs, and other commercial uses. Many town and country communities have commercial forests and wood-processing plants as their economic base or a prominent part of it. Timber from farm woodlots makes up a special raw material from lands generally thought of solely in terms of crops and livestock.

Outdoor recreation has been a prominent aspect of town and country for generations. It is growing steadily under the pressure of demand. Outdoor Recreation Resources Review Commission (ORRRC) studies show 283 million acres of public recreation areas in the United States, Puerto Rico, and the Virgin Islands. Privately owned recreational or potentially recreational lands exceed the public areas and represent both recreational resources and economic opportunities for the owners.

Town and Country People and Their Communities

The U. S. farm population in 1965 (including family members) was about 12.4 million. According to 1960 census definitions it consists of persons residing on places of 10 acres or more from which at least $50 worth of farm products were sold in the preceding year and on places of less than 10 acres from which at least $250 worth of products were sold. During 1964—65 almost a million people left farms or discontinued production; at the same time about 275,000 moved to farms or were on places that became farms.[3] It is noteworthy that in one year many people become farmers though the total number of farmers shows a larger net decrease.

It is important not to equate the farm population with the rural population of which it is a part. Newspapers and reports of social scientists have presented articles and statistics on the "farm population decline," from which churchmen sometimes have generalized erroneously a "town and country population decline."

Another segment of the population in town and country is made up of rural nonfarm residents. This classification came into usage by the Bureau of Census in 1930. Rural nonfarm people live in open country, villages, small towns, and along highways. They are blue- and white-collar workers, business and professional people, artists and industrialists, part-time employees and retirees. This segment of the population is growing rapidly, especially within a radius from the more populous areas.

In addition to the farm and rural nonfarm sectors, the town and country population includes those who reside in larger towns and small cities. In these communities are retail establishments, wholesale firms, distribution houses, small and large industries. Many of these small industries have both national and international distribution. Large industries, such as mining operations, may employ several thousand persons from several counties.

Town and country people are not sure whether they belong to the urban or the rural sector of society. They find that their community is not rural. It is over 2,500. To call it urban, at 3 or 4 thousand, seems incongruous with common meanings attached to the word. Yet the rural classification is not big enough today for many countryside residents or their towns and cities. Both terms appear to be obsolete.

The Quest for Identity

The lack of certainty as to where they fit in the traditional rural-urban framework reflects itself in the relationships of town and country communities. In some ways a town of 3,000 will consider itself quite apart from neighboring smaller communities with which it has a common geographical setting and economic base; in other ways it will identify with them. An agricultural service center of 10 or 20 thousand will go to great lengths to emulate a major city and at times play down (by omission or disavowal) its interdependence with "rural" towns and open country; at other times it will champion its relationship with the hinterland. There appears to be a split personality among town and country communities as to who they are and with whom they identify.

In the present situation town and country communities are in something of a crisis of identity. They are involved in transition themselves in the framework of radical changes of society at large. Town and country communities and their citizens are somewhat nameless. They are at a turning point in self-identification, not sure whether the terms of the Bureau of Census and the sociologists fit or not. At the same time their friends and relatives in the large cities are quite certain of the urban label.

Even though the census calls them urban, many people in a community of 4 or 5 thousand, or 10 or 12 thousand for that matter, do not consider themselves urbanites. To call them rural may constitute a considerable social affront. Town and country, though in familiar usage by the churches, has not been widely used by communities and their citizens in nonmetropolitan counties as a word for community and personal identification.

The term town and country has advantages and possibilities, but a better may emerge. Nonmetropolitan is a word that has grown alongside metropolitan. Its disadvantage lies in reflecting what town and country is not. While it has a negative prefix, the limits of language may force its adoption. A name with broad acceptance is needed and may be found or invented. Until one emerges some confusion will continue.

Church Involvement Reflected

The church is involved in the life and concerns of people who live in town and country. Except for the Catholics, who immigrated mainly to the cities, the establishment of congregations took place largely in the towns, villages, and open country. People from Protestant lands took up farming, ranching, and Main Street business occupations in the prime agricultural areas. Their congregations and churches were close to them in their struggles. As urbanization develops, denominations may underestimate the mission of the church in town and country.

Recent publications reflect efforts of churchmen to analyze and to come to grips with the problems and responsibilities: *A Time of Decision for People in the Great Plains, Death and Birth of the Parish, Ferment on the Fringe,*

Inside Rural America: A Lutheran View, It's Bright in My Valley, New Thousands in Town and Country, Mission in the American Outdoors, On Good Soil, Our Church Meeting Human Needs, The Church and Faith in Mid-America, The Larger Parish and Group Ministry, and *The Silent Struggle for Mid-America.* Such books and other media can further the dialog and thought needed to strengthen the church in mission to all men.

Town and country conferences, institutes, seminars, and workshops contribute to the discussion. Christians of all denominations are studying—within their respective denominations and interdenominationally—the church's structures and performance as well as socioeconomic developments. August W. Engelbrecht has edited the findings of Lutheran study meetings held from 1945 to 1962 and has written *Ideas for Church Leaders for Town and Country Areas.*

"A reading of the brief accounts of the workshops reveals that in each instance," its Foreword relates, "the study process is tailor-made for the particular geographical and social situation. Patterns of church mission are not imposed from without. Rather patterns that grow out of the needs of the areas are encouraged.

"Varying answers to similar problems in different geographical areas are given. They are the result of laymen and pastors conscientiously dealing with realities in search for workable solutions. Small group discussions in workshops open the way to problem solving through the exchange of information, ideas and alternate courses of action."

What comes of workshop efforts to deal with issues and problems in town and country? For one thing, attitudes change. Said a Nebraska wheatgrower in 1966: "For a long while I was under the impression that the church was forgetting about us. Forgetting people in the small towns and rural areas. I wasn't at our workshop. Wasn't able to get there. But I read the report carefully. And it carries a lot of good ideas. I began to realize that the church-at-large cares about what's happening and what we can do together."

The attitudes of many pastors are affected. Pastors who serve town and country parishes sometimes come to feel that where they are serving is held in less esteem by others. The study and workshop approach has helped some of them develop a tougher skin. Charles DeVries interviewed various individuals in the preparation of *Inside Rural America: A Lutheran View*. He asked a group of rural Iowa pastors, "Do you still get the rather insinuating question, 'Are you *still* in Jonesville? Are you *still* in Corn Grove?'" To the general affirmative response, "Yes," they added, "But now there's a difference. It no longer bothers us."

Leaders of church in town and country regard the land-grant universities a prime resource for study. The influence of continuing education conferences for town and country clergy (interdenominational) at land-grant universities contributes toward a positive view. In traveling to a meeting to plan the succeeding year's Town and Country Church Leaders Conference a pastor shared his thoughts: "When I finished seminary I accepted the idea of serving in a small town, with the prospect of moving on to better things. During last year's town and country conference I began to see things differently. Things I'd missed in our county, in our town, were discussed by the university faculty in such a way that they came alive. I was honestly anxious to get home to work with the information and insights gained. What was given bore out well in practice. Whenever a call to another parish may come, and a move is appropriate, I'll be as open to another town and country parish as to that of a city or suburb."

Such a response is wholesome and reflects a highly desired balance of interest in each sector of our society — city, suburb, and countryside.

2 New Dimensions of Town and Country

Early Americans built their businesses, farms, and professions—their institutions and communities—on relatively small geographical bases. The development of technology for the agricultural, manufacturing, communications, and transportation industries opened the way for larger dimensions of life and work that both town and country and urban citizens now enjoy.

Discoveries, inventions, and technological advances in either setting soon and pervasively affected the other. For example, automobiles and trucks developed in the cities were readily used in rural areas. Agricultural mechanization developed in rural areas released millions of people from rudimentary agriculture to help meet the growing urban needs of labor and management. The energetic and inventive capacities of the urban and rural populations benefited and stimulated each other. Perhaps in no other country has the interpenetration and interdependence of urban and rural populations been so broad, continuous, and influential.

In both urban and town and country areas earlier patterns of livelihood, institutional development, and governmental function are being exposed to and challenged by new and continuing opportunities, problems, and responsibilities.

Change and expansion in metropolitan areas tend to be dramatic and frequently are brought into view through various media. Developments in nonmetropolitan areas are more difficult to perceive and have less visibility in mass media.

Wider Relationships in Town and Country

Town and country areas are not at a standstill. Growth and decline, development and deterioration — both seen and hardly recognized — are on the scene. Town and country communities are quite unlike what they were a generation, a decade, or even a year ago. "Hometown" for each of us is never quite what it was yesterday.

In the fall of 1965, during a break from discing wheatland near the Minot Air Force Base in North Dakota, a wheatgrower and a visitor exchanged reflections concerning changes in that area of the Great Plains.

"I remember," said the wheatgrower, "when a person could stand at this corner of the field and yell loud enough to be heard at once by people at four farmsteads. Now one could yell all day, and likely no one may hear him at all."

Pointing progressively in each of four directions, he remarked, "A house and family were there until 1939. There till 1946. There till 1949. There till 1951."

Of the four farmsteads not a building — neither house nor barn — remained.

"They've gone to Glenburn, Minot, Minneapolis, and elsewhere," he said. "These places were settled on the 160-acre units provided by the Homestead Act of 1862. A piece of ground that size doesn't fit farming in the Dakotas these days. Maybe it really never did."

The disappearance of four farmsteads with the inclusion of the small units into a larger one represents expansion in town and country. Accompanying the expansion of farm size (and for similar reasons) is an increase in the scope of life and work from single community and county levels to that of several communities and counties.

A number of small communities situated in four counties of North Dakota — Bottineau, McHenry, Renville, and Ward — live in relation to one another. All have a common interdependence with Minot to the south, population 30,000, as a major service center; however, they share economic and social activity somewhat distinct from Minot. Glenburn is central in this area, being the location of a telephone exchange, having a consolidated school, and providing several businesses and farm equipment enterprises.

Glenburn, in relation to the open country and villages around it, has a noteworthy present and promising future. Citizens and community leaders are working to develop their town as a desirable place to live. It shares in the community improvement program of the state. The homes, institutions, streets, and general appearance of

Glenburn indicate development and expansion—town and country style.

A visit to smaller surrounding villages, though these are declining in population and in the number of business establishments, reveals a concern for life and service of a high quality. These communities, together with Glenburn, are an example of an expanding network of villages, towns, and farms that make up what may be called an area community.

Lutheran congregations in the four-county Glenburn area have formed a study committee to explore ways that may provide worship and education facilities, ministry, outreach, and coordination of work that fit the new situation. The Lutheran Church in America, The American Lutheran Church, and The Lutheran Church—Missouri Synod have congregations in the area. Three laymen of each national church group compose a nine-man study committee with the ministers as pastoral advisers.

The committee is exploring ideas and alternative courses of action that may best meet the twin demands for the most adequate parish program and for facilities built with the wisest use of resources. Area workshops, exchange visits, joint services of worship, and informal discussions are some of the means by which members are broadening and deepening their familiarity with the overall situation.

A nonprofit corporation, based on the members or the congregations of the area, that could build and hold title to a single church plant with education and worship facilities has been studied. The committee's goal is to find ways, respecting the experience and traditions of each congregation, to assure the most adequate parish program. While there is some desire to construct new buildings, to replace those that are spent, the committee cautions the congregations not to build. An area concept and facilities that meet both the short-term needs and the long-term goals of all congregations in the area are two primary factors guiding the study committee.

Economic Areas in the Countryside

Persons who seek to understand town and country today may find a relatively new network of economic areas to be of prime significance.

A need has long existed to identify areas made up of several counties having natural, economic, and social factors in common. Already around 1940 the U. S. Bureau of Census was aware of this need, and in 1949 it used multicounty units as a basis of some of its census reporting.

The 1950 Census of Population, Agriculture, and Housing used a system of economic provinces, regions, subregions, and state economic areas developed by Donald J. Bogue and Calvin L. Beale under the combined sponsorship of the Bureau of Census and the U. S. Department of Agriculture.[4] Bogue and Beale identified 5 economic provinces, 13 economic regions, 121 economic subregions, and 506 state economic areas.

In this system the basic units are "state economic areas," groupings of several counties. Each economic area is named and described to provide a basis for analyzing multicounty areas that have a number of fundamental characteristics in common. "The principal goal is to show the distinctive ways by which the inhabitants of the respective parts of the Nation earn their living, using a minimum number of categories of area to portray a maximum picture of differences."[5]

A relatively new force at work in town and country is altering provincial interests of single communities. It is the experience and realization that the best interests and development opportunities of a community lie in being leagued with surrounding villages, towns, and small cities. County and multicounty planning groups are being formed to the benefit of an entire area. The work of Bogue and Beale is particularily helpful for understanding a community, county, and state economic area in terms of potential development and of the relation to subregion, region, province, and nation.

Using the information and the names of state economic areas may prove to be helpful in the quest for identity. Area names are being used by promotion groups in numerous settings of the country and are being adopted into the vocabulary of town and country residents. Often area terms are cited, in preference to the names of particular communities or counties, to identify places of residence and socioeconomic activity.

Churchmen need to be aware of state economic areas. Congregations were formed on the basis of small neighborhoods and communities decades and generations ago. To carry on the ministries and outreach the Gospel calls for, familiarity with the larger dimensions of economic and social life is necessary. While the structures of the world do not determine the content of the church's work, the world's structures have much to say about how the church tools its own structures for mission and service.

Two congregations in Iowa, for example, left their respective declining communities to consolidate and serve a larger population base with new facilities in the open country near intersecting highways. This is not to suggest that congregations in small towns will do better merely by leaving. Rather it is to suggest that mission planning calls for optimum use of socioeconomic information. As people take part in larger associations of society, there is need for congregations to address themselves to the larger scene.

Elements Basic to Area Churchmanship

A booklet of devotions for church council meetings was recently published by the Evangelism Committee of the Nebraska Synod, Lutheran Church in America. One of the writers, a medical doctor, tells what a certain patient once said to his doctor: "Doctor, I don't just want to survive. Help me to live."

Congregations in various town and country areas of the United States echo the plaintive cry of that patient: "We don't just want to survive. Help us to live."

Despite a theology that terms the Christian church an organic entity in which the parts relate in life-sharing functions, many congregations in town and country tend not to know one another. Despite the creedal expression, "I believe in . . . the communion of saints," the saints tend to remain quite restricted to their own congregations. Too often the congregation tends to be something of a solo flight.

While denominations espouse ecumenical relationships, many church agencies serve congregations largely on the basis of straight-line, unilateral relationships. Time for exploring the common experiences and mission of the Christ-centered congregations, in an economic area or even in a county, is consumed in denominational concerns. Denominational mission needs to be in balance with the common mission of Christians at the local level. Singular denominational approaches help congregations to survive. But the question of community life—the essence of which is human relationships—needs to be raised.

Annual meetings of congregations are critical junctures at which to examine the mission of a congregation or group of congregations. So often the question is merely: "How are we doing? Is our congregation doing all right?" Larger and more appropriate questions might be: "How well are congregations in the county pursuing the common mission? What is taking place in our county or economic area? What are the unmet needs of people? How might congregations work together to strengthen Christian ministry and service in society?"

Presentations by a study committee, laymen and pastors of other denominations, or panel discussions (both lay and clergy) on what denominations are doing individually and in coordination with others may help to nurture Christian growth. Relevant discussion on the mission of the church in a county or a state economic area takes imagination on the part of laymen and pastors. Fortunately innovativeness is a gift widely given.

Elements for developing an area concept of Christian mission may be expressed in many ways. The following may be helpful:

1. Openness to learning from community leaders and public resources.

2. Openness of church members to the presence and purpose of other congregations.

3. Openness of pastors to the presence and purpose of other pastors.

4. Openness in seeking the well-being of all congregations in an area toward their being strengthened to serve.

Area churchmanship requires a larger view of life than the parochial self-interest congregations sometimes succumb to. It requires a world view. A world view tells us, as Helmut Thielicke says, "something about the ultimate meaning of life and the world."[6] A congregation that discovers the meaning of its existence in God's purposes for the world is capable of area churchmanship. A

28

congregation that has lost, or has not discovered, a world view as the larger context of its ministry tends to regard the common mission either as pointless or as a threat. In town and country, and perhaps in other settings, congregations struggle with the tension between a limiting congregational view and the larger context of life.

The State as a Community

Each of the states in America is somewhat a community of diverse communities. States bring together the interests of metropolitan centers and nonmetropolitan counties. State boundaries span urban-versus-rural gaps.

One of the significant developments of our time is the degree to which urban people participate in activity that brings them to town and country areas and a corresponding increase of activity that brings people of the villages, towns, and small cities to the urban centers. There are fewer citizens today whose lives can be characterized as solely urban or rural.

Millions of urban residents have lived a substantial part of their lives in town and country. More and more urban people, including those who do not have a farm or town and country background, participate in activities of the countryside — through second homes in resort communities, farm vacations, fishing and hunting trips, and other forms of recreation and tourism. Occupational commitments of many urban residents in business, education, government, industry, the professions, and social agencies also bring them into town and country regularly. Elements of residence and occupations often are instrumental in extending the outlook and social concerns of city people from narrow urban to broader statewide interests.

Town and country people too, in pursuit of both leisure-time activity and occupational enterprise, live with one foot in the country and one in the city, although most of the weight is determined by the place of residence.

Farmers, ranchers, and rural nonfarm residents spend considerable time in enjoying the cultural, educational, shopping, and recreational opportunities cities offer. Professional sports, theater, and music events are attended by "country cousins" who may tie in such activities with an invited stay with relatives or elect the privacy and luxurious accommodations of a city's hotels or motels. Occupational commitments of town and country people in agriculture, business, education, government, industry, the professions, and social agencies bring them into the cities regularly. Participation in the life of the city often stimulates town and country people to forsake narrow rural interests in favor of the larger perspective of the well-being of all.

Social and economic conditions of a state are reflected in both urban and town and country settings. A state that has little concern for its cities is not acting wisely. Nor is one that neglects or takes for granted its town and country areas. In all states the cities and the countryside have basic concerns and problems in common.

Agencies Serve Statewide Community

Public agencies of service exemplify ways in which the common interests of urban and rural people are interwoven. Soil and Water Conservation Districts (and agricultural experiment stations) have prepared statewide soil surveys, carefully mapping soil types and capabilities. This has been done to meet basic agricultural needs which are at once in the interest of the entire society. As urban and suburban land developments expand, the value of the soil maps for urban land utilization is coming increasingly into view. Septic tanks do not function in nonporous soils. Nor is a housing development on a floodplain a wise investment.

The Cooperative Extension Service, based in the state land-grant universities, conducts an adult education program that is respected and emulated by many nations. This service agency is a partnership of national, state, and county governments that conducts out-of-school educational programs for urban and rural people in all counties. Under state directors of extension, county extension agents serve approximately 32 percent of the low-income people, 31 percent of the farm people, and 39 percent of the "urban" (communities of 2,500 and over) people in the United States.

Statewide service is rendered also by state economic development agencies in all 50 states as well as Puerto Rico and the Virgin Islands. These agencies have a consultative and resource role for development in cities and town and country. Contact with them and a reading of their literature (news bulletins and reports) reveal that they have concern for all counties and communities. These agencies are being strengthened to help develop agriculture, business, communities, small and large industries, and outdoor recreation and tourism.

Denominations and congregations do well to increase their knowledge of statewide service agencies. These agencies have programs and personnel that can be a significant resource to church groups. From time to time state leaders in public agencies express appreciation for being in touch with church leaders or express a desire to do so. This receptivity presents a basis for dialog with public educators and decision makers that may not be sufficiently known or shared in by state and local church leaders.

31

Developing Capacities to Relate to Regions

Diversity characterizes the climate, topography, population, and economic pursuits of the countryside. Superficial observation may cause one to lump all cities together or to assume a monotonous sameness about town and country communities. But it simply is not true that all cities are the same. Nor is it true that to know one rural town is to know them all.

Knowledge of the region in which a city or town and country community is situated provides a framework for understanding a community's style of life and socioeconomic functions. Even within regions these vary greatly. Too often church leaders impose upon a community, its citizens and institutions, an analysis and evaluation based not on what is valid from within but on factors external to it. A church leader from a large city once roundly criticized a gathering of congregations on the Great Plains for their meager performance in stewardship. Unknown to him, it was during a period of low cattle and grain prices. The failure to do his homework and the tactless approach accomplished the opposite of what he intended. His appearance became a burden to the congregations conscientiously seeking to perform their best despite the current economic realities.

Parish pastors, laymen, and seminary professors are seeking to become familiar with the social and economic realities within multistate regions through continuing education conferences, institutes, seminars, and schools for town and country leaders at the land-grant universities. About 28 of these are held throughout the United States on an annual basis; 2 or 3 are held every 2 years. These continuing education events are interdenominational and exemplify a constructive relationship of church and state. State universities find it within their proper role to use facilities and faculties to share educational information with churchmen as one of their publics.

An interfaith committee has broadened the concept of continuing education through state of society conferences. These are major study events for church administrators and church staff personnel (interdenominational) who have responsibility for town and country. The committee's officers reflect the breadth of leadership in this endeavor: Dr. Paul C. Johnson, chairman, editorial director of the *Prairie Farmer;* Dr. E. W. Mueller, associate secretary, Department of Church and Community Planning, Lutheran Council in the U. S. A.; Msgr. E. W. O'Rourke, first vice-chairman, National Catholic Rural Life Conference; Dr. J. B. Claar, second vice-chairman, state director of Illinois Cooperative Extension Service; and Dr. Phillip F. Aylesworth, consultant, Program Relationships, U. S. Department of Agriculture.

The initial state of society conference was held for the Northern Great Plains — Colorado, Kansas, Montana, Nebraska, North Dakota, South Dakota, and Wyoming. Social scientists of each of the seven land-grant universities of these states combined forces to bring church leaders a comprehensive up-to-date analysis of what is happening and what appears on the horizon. The event was held in November 1964 at the University of Nebraska's Center for Continuing Education. Major considerations of the 3-day conference were the function of religion in society, an overview of the region, analyses and implications of trends, and a probing for directions in which answers lie.

The significance of continuing education at land-grant universities (for pastors, seminary professors, and laymen annually or every 2 years and for church administrators and church staff every 5 or 10 years) lies in several areas. First, it is high-caliber continuing education for professional leaders available throughout the nation. Second, it provides an opportunity for open dialog by social scientists and church leaders who have a common concern for society. Third, it becomes an occasion when church leaders discover ways to relate to and utilize public resources. Finally, it broadens and deepens the familiarity of church leaders, on an interdenominational basis, with the nature and significance of the various regions and states.

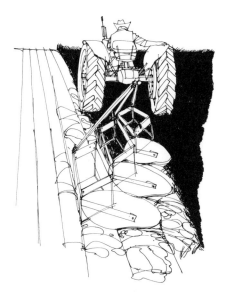

3
Agriculture and the Welfare of the Nation

Through diverse and productive agriculture, town and country areas of the U.S. and Canada make vital contributions to their respective populations and economies. Agriculture—based on natural resources and developed through human ingenuity—has produced foods so well for so long that most citizens have never known a critical national food shortage. This is not the case in most other countries.

American agriculture is a capable provider and a

major employer. Our agriculture and agribusiness provide a variety of about 5,000 different foods. Agriculture employs about 6 million workers, more than the automobile, steel, public utility, and transportation industries combined. Because of agricultural productivity most citizens are free from the necessity of growing foodstuff to pursue other enterprises. In Russia, where 108 million of 232 million people live in rural areas, a far larger proportion is engaged in food production. There one farmer produces enough food for about nine other people. The American farmer produces enough for about 33.

Looking Beyond the Supermarket

Theological perspectives encourage society's concern for agriculture and agriculture's concern for society. In his discussion of the Lord's Prayer, Helmut Thielicke invites us to perceive the significance of basic values. "If the Lord's Prayer were not so familiar to us, if we had not so often looked through this prism, then surely this shaft of light that falls upon our daily bread would strike us as strange and astonishing.

"I think we ought to . . . reexamine our whole scale of values so far as our vital needs are concerned. If we do this—and the 'idealists' among us, especially, might well do this—we shall very soon discover that it is precisely the 'little things' and among them our 'daily bread,' that occupy a very high priority." [7]

Through soils and waters of the earth and through the workaday efforts of millions of people engaged in agricultural pursuits, God grants the recurring grace of daily bread.

Soil scientists tell us that a thimbleful of healthy topsoil has more living microorganisms in it than there are people in the United States. The created gift of topsoil strikes the imagination even more emphatically when we

36

learn that the microorganisms in a thimbleful of topsoil conduct a wider variety of activities than all the people in the manifold job classifications in the U.S. All people on earth are dependent on the earth's thin 6 inches of topsoil.

The large supply of fertile soil on this continent is a basic reason we eat so well. Whether our agricultural soils will be conserved and developed for meeting increased demands in the future is an open question. Highways, housing developments, and general urban sprawl are fast preempting thousands of acres of our best farmland.

Without rich soils and abundant waters — together with responsible use of them — no corn or potatoes, meat or milk could be assured us by the grocer, distributor, processor, economist, or government official. Beyond the supermarket lie the soils and flow the waters — God's creation for man's wise use.

Theologians are increasingly interested in the relation of man to the physical world. During a study meeting on conservation of natural resources at the continuing education center of the University of Chicago, Joseph Haroutunian opened his remarks on Christian concern for nature with this comment: "You would be surprised what big areas we theologians are able to ignore." He went on to criticize the idea that man becomes autonomous from nature through civilization. He asked, "How do you get civilized man to recognize that he exists by transaction with the physical world, or that it is in the physical world that he truly does exist as a human being?"

People, as well as "mother earth," are behind the shelves that display attractively packaged food products. We may tend to forget them and their needs. People in occupations other than our own are remembered even in our liturgy when we pray in a "Prayer of the Church": "Take under thy special protection those whose toil is difficult or dangerous, and be with all who lay their hands to any useful task. Give them just rewards for their labor, and the knowledge that their work is good in thy sight, who art the Maker and Sustainer of all things."

A veritable army makes the growing, harvest, and distribution of our food possible. Over 3 million farmers and ranchers produce the raw materials for our widespread food industry. "Three out of every ten jobs in private employment are related to agriculture. Six million people have jobs providing the supplies farmers use for production and family living. Eight to ten million people have jobs storing, transporting, processing, and merchandising the products of agriculture."[8] Add to these the people in agricultural research and education at the high school, college, and graduate levels.

Relating Farm and City People

The dimensions of employment and the variety of functions in agriculture and agribusiness illustrate the interaction and interdependence of farm and city people in our economy. Without skilled people in farming and ranching, marketing, processing, distribution, and retailing the people of our nation would have to spend much of their time growing and processing their own food. If this were so, technological progress, industrial production, education, and other pursuits would be greatly cut back. On the other hand, the producers of food are dependent on researchers, educators, engineers, suppliers of machinery, people in the life sciences, and providers of credit. Were it not for these services, available on a continuous basis, American agriculture would revert to rudimentary levels.

Relationships in the organism of society are multiplex. Each "organ" lives in relation with, benefits from, and contributes to the whole. It is not wise to separate metropolitan and town and country populations, either by default or by contrived means. If any segment of society is left out of the mainstream, stagnation tends to set in. This is also true of the church as an organism. It is not wise for the church to separate metropolitan and town and country memberships. In interaction we live. In separateness both tend to stagnate for lack of relationship, stimulation, and the creative force of meeting others somewhat unlike ourselves.

Urban and town and country people—those in the business and industry of metropolitan centers and those in farming, ranching, lumbering, and allied enterprises in rural areas—need each other in order to build and sustain a comprehensive experience and view of society. Without such interaction even our language regarding other segments of society degenerates into lazy caricatures. It is appalling to hear an urban person, whose mind is closed to agriculture and rural life, speak disparagingly of small town and open country. It is equally appalling to hear castigations of the city and urban life from a rural resident whose world view is similarly stunted. "Language [is] more than a means," Aarne Siirala reminds us in *The Voice of Illness.* "It represents a particular way of building up the world."

The church, the communion of saints, has motivation in the Gospel—the compulsion of its mission—to encourage and stimulate communication between people of all segments of society. Christian faith desires and seeks reconciliation among men and with the earth. In his prison letters Dietrich Bonhoeffer wrote: "God, our brother, and the earth belong together. Without God, without his brother, man loses the earth. . . . There is no way back to the earth except the way to God and to our brother."

The Lord's Prayer and the Apostles' Creed, explanations of them in the Small Catechism, the Biblical accounts of Creation, the prophets, psalms, parables of Jesus, some of the epistles, and the liturgy—all give ample theological vantage points for discussion of basic values and goals for relating metropolitan and nonmetropolitan concerns and needs.

Basic Factors in Agricultural Development

On May 15, 1862, President Abraham Lincoln signed a bill that created the United States Department of Agriculture. In his Message to Congress in 1864 he said: "The Agriculture Department . . . is rapidly commending itself to the great and vital interest it was created to advance. It is peculiarly the people's department, in which they feel more directly concerned than in any other."

Before the department came into being, many men had made vital contributions toward its emergence. In Alfred Stefferud's words they were "the discoverers, explorers, colonists and pioneers; yes. After them the farmers, inventors, scientists, administrators. The seeds they sowed were great, but we need not use that label for them, because to Nature one seed is not greater than another. What counts, in total, is a symbiosis, in which different organisms live, work, and progress in an association that is of advantage to all." [9]

In preparation for the centennial of the Department of Agriculture, leaders in government and in private life regarded it as "fitting that we count the blessings which we all enjoy as a result of 100 years of agricultural progress" and recognize "the spiritual resources which have made our agricultural progress possible." In response to a request from those who were planning the centennial Wendell Belew, Southern Baptist Convention; Henry A. McCanna, National Council of the Churches of Christ in the U. S. A.; E. W. Mueller, Lutheran Council in the U. S. A.; and Edward W. O'Rourke, National Catholic

Rural Life Conference, coauthored *The Church and Agricultural Progress,* which was published by the Department of Agriculture. In it the churchmen reflect Biblical concepts in relation to agriculture: "America has been blessed with abundant agricultural production, based on rich resources of land and human creativity. Behind the given natural and human resources stands the benevolent Creator.

"When people from many nations came to settle this vast continent, they found fertile soil and favorable climate. In this new land, they could sow their knowledge of plant and animal life in order to harvest life-sustaining food and fiber for man.

"From the beginning of our nation to the present man has been able to increase the productivity of resources from agriculture by discovering, describing and working with laws created and governed by God for the benefit of mankind. These laws or principles pertain as much to the internal combustion engine as they do to the genetic traits of a certain plant. The mystery of electricity and the ecology of the microorganisms of the soil both contribute in a special way to agricultural production. But both are governed by God.

"Basing its enterprise on the given Creation, American agriculture has been able to advance the production of food to such a degree as to supply the nation abundantly and to give encouragement to the peoples of the world.

"The bounty that springs from our verdant fields is not solely the product of an industrious and inventive people. Man does not work alone."

The Task Ahead for Agriculture

Farming and ranching, agricultural marketing, and food processing and distribution will more and more be public concerns in the years ahead. For the past two decades abundant land, water, and agricultural commodities have appeared to offer no major worry for the average citizen. As the supply of each of these tightens on the national and world scene, public interest will heighten.

Farm organizations themselves will bring agriculture increasingly into public view through local, state, regional, and national conferences and public forums. The farm organizations — American Farm Bureau Federation, National Farmers Organization, National Farmers Union, National Farm Workers Association, and the National Grange — are becoming more keenly aware of the importance of public opinion. Demonstrations of collective bargaining in agriculture (livestock and milk holding actions or grape worker strikes) command wide coverage in mass media. These help farm people tell their story. But many members and leaders of farm organizations want a continuous flow of information in public media about the job being done and the enlarging role of agriculture on the national and world scene. Once content to speak almost solely to themselves, people in agriculture are coming to realize that issues must be shared in the public marketplace of information.

Academic leaders, publishers, professional groups, and various trade journals are studying agriculture and the needs for food and fiber. The receptivity of churchmen to state of society conferences and the growing participation of clergy and laymen in continuing education events at land-grant universities indicate a concern for agriculture and for life in nonmetropolitan areas among American religious leaders. It is noteworthy that Pope John XXIII's *Mater et Magistra,* on Christianity and social progress, discusses world agriculture and rural life at some length. The writer of a study outline for the encyclical, published by the Paulist Press, states that the "welfare of mankind depends in large measure upon the state of agriculture; should this fail to provide the necessary food and fiber, the plight of industrial and urban dwellers would be serious."

Projections into the future indicate the need to increase, not to reduce, agriculture production. In his study of the needs in *Agriculture and the Public Interest* Leon H. Keyserling writes: "Taking into account both needed improvements in diets and population growth, and comparing 1975 with 1964, our domestic requirements for increased farm products are very great. Meat utilization should rise 27 percent; dairy products, 25 percent; fruits, 53 percent; and vegetables, 37 percent. Even potatoes should rise 20 percent; and wheat 8 percent. Cotton use should rise 21 percent."

Keyserling adds: "How much should our exports of farm products be encouraged to rise, if we are to draw upon the true productive capabilities of American agriculture in making our fair contribution toward the war against poverty and hunger, discontent and ferment, around the world? Again comparing 1975 with 1964, and including commercial exports as well as those in the form of aid, our exports of red meat should be nearly nine times as high in 1975 as in 1964; dairy products, almost ten times as high; food fats and oils, about double; wheat, about 50 percent higher, and cotton more than double.

"Combining our real domestic needs and desirable export goals, and even assuming the exclusion of Communist Asia from these export goals, the total utilization of U. S. farm products should be 35 percent higher in 1975 than in 1964 for red meat; 46 percent for dairy products; 51 percent for fruits; 37 percent for vegetables; 49 percent for food fats and oils; 31 percent for wheat; 56 percent for corn; and 52 percent for cotton. If Communist Asia were to be included within the range of our export efforts by 1975, the total utilization of our domestic production would be even higher by 1975."

The task ahead for agriculture does not consist of food and fiber production alone. Agriculture itself must so administer its own affairs that it keeps pace with society at large. It must keep pace in terms of economic, educational, research and development, and social needs. Agricultural leaders—farmers, ranchers, suppliers, educators, farm organization people, and social scientists—must work together to win for agriculture the profit it needs to meet the increasing demands of society.

Agriculture has need to deepen its social concerns, to play a more creative and sustaining role in education, and to assist town and country communities and institutions to both adjust and develop according to new situations that are thrust onto the scene by rapidly moving technology.

Career opportunities are rather plentiful in agriculture and agribusiness. Deans of the colleges of agriculture at the land-grant universities throughout the United States report that the demand for people with undergraduate and graduate degrees in agriculture and agribusiness exceeds the supply by no small margin. Three factors contribute to this shortage. First, agricultural leaders, including the land-grant universities, have not been getting substantive information to the public. (This is a particularly important function.) Second, farmers and ranchers themselves, for one reason or another, have not often enough seen the multiple opportunities in agriculture and agribusiness for their own children. (They do well to heed Theodore Roosevelt's advice that each profession ought to take time to recruit for its own ranks.) Third, too often high school teachers and guidance counselors (overinfluenced by headline thinking about "the decline of the farm population") have failed to point out the opportunities in professional farming and agribusiness.

One urgent task that faces agricultural leaders is to find ways to encourage and achieve a widespread influx of young people into the diverse, numerous, and demanding careers in modern agriculture. There are problems aplenty for youth to tackle with their characteristic energy and idealism.

A problem of great magnitude that is not yet fully in view or not yet adequately assessed is whether the world's mounting population can be adequately fed. In most of the underveloped countries 60 to 80 percent of the people are in farming, but their production is so low they cannot meet the needs of their own populations. Industrialization is thought to be the rapid road to affluence. But industrialization cannot come without first providing for the adequate and continuous foods needed for improved nourishment and efficiency. American agriculture has two approaches that apply to the problem: assistance in developing the agriculture of underdeveloped countries; food supplies through aid and trade programs.

A dimension of American agriculture in its task within our economy is its growing export performance and its importance in the balance of payments. A publication of the U. S. Department of Agriculture, *Foreign Agriculture* (Aug. 15, 1966), says: "Thanks entirely to an increase in commercial sales for dollars, U. S. agricultural exports reached a record-breaking $6.7 billion in fiscal 1965–66, exceeding the previous fiscal year record by $600 million. This large gain in agricultural exports contributed significantly to narrowing the U. S. balance-of-payment gap."

Solution of a Major Problem Needed

The farmer and the rancher have achieved dramatic increases in the much-heralded value that Americans place on efficiency. Yet their efficiency and productivity have not brought them the economic return that generates in other segments of the economy.

One of the arguments leveled against the farm income problem has been that of the various strata of size and efficiency of farm operations. This explanation has merit; yet an overview of farm income reflects a perennial problem. In his study of *Farms and Farmers in an Urban Age* Edward Higbee says: "One of the strangest features of modern agriculture is that farm income stagnated during the years when technical efficiency made some of its greatest gains. In the decade 1948—59 production per man-hour on farms increased 48.6 percent while the improvement in other industries was only 25.5 percent. In 1959 the average income of all farm families from agriculture was $2,875 while that of urban families was $5,911. In that same year 18 percent of all farm families had a total income of less than $1,000 whereas only 3 percent of all urban families had such inadequate incomes."

Higbee points out that this "lumps all farmers together." He goes on to raise the question whether many minimal producers should be classified as farmers.

What may speak currently to the problem of farm income is the frequency with which productive farmers are dropping out in favor of more remunerative pursuits. In the period Higbee describes, people leaving agriculture tended to be marginal producers. What farm papers, trade periodicals, and visits in farm areas now reveal is a concern over the number of relatively efficient farmers, especially dairymen, who are calling it quits. Some dairymen, on computing their income on an hourly basis, find themselves supplying the labor, investment, management, and risk all for 65 or 70 cents an hour in an occupation that demands 365 days per year. They wonder whether the privilege of providing milk on such a basis is worth it.

Milk shortages may become sharp in various parts of the country. In spite of a recent increase in milk subsidy, many dairymen may discontinue, which in turn may bring on milk shortages. Perhaps the situation must become critical before price and income rise to the point that assures an adequate number of milk sources. Income needs for farmers on a substantial long-term basis, corresponding to income in other segments of the economy, must be realized, or many capable farmers will shift to other occupations. If the consuming public wants a plentiful supply of dairy products, price and income for the farmer must be a paying proposition.

What the modern farmer brings to his profession merits an income commensurate with that of other high-level investment, management, and labor input enterprises. Some analysts point out that farmers in part tend to bring price and income problems on themselves. They have given much attention to production and too little to marketing. Perhaps they have been too ready to discount their own labor, provided they could make some return on investment.

Farm service agencies, too, have tended to be largely production oriented. While improvement in production is important, the more neglected factor of marketing demands the concentrated attention of farmers, educators, market specialists, and private and public agencies. Long-term public interests are related to agricultural marketing. If marketing fails the producer of food and fiber, in the long run it will eventually fail the consumer as well.

Farmers have been advised to take several courses of action in order to achieve economic goals. The factor of efficiency has had more advocates than any other. This is no time to discredit efficiency. It has an essential role. Many speak for a free reign of supply and demand. This is no time to discredit the basic logic of supply and demand. Nothing can replace the fundamental aspects of this economic reality. Many regard cooperative buying and selling as the answer for the farmer. Great gains have been made through cooperatives. This function is within the circumference of beneficial agricultural economics. Proponents of collective bargaining in agricultural marketing have stimulated agricultural thought out of some listless drifting. In a world of pluralistic centers of power, responsible use of collective bargaining has a contribution to make. Another segment of agriculture wants government to take the lead and provide the economic framework in which agriculture is to operate, plus much of the financial substance. Few would challenge the idea that government has a role to play.

What seems inadequate and unsatisfactory is when any single approach is dominant and is relied on too heavily by itself. Advocates of particular approaches tend to become doctrinaire, offering patent medicine. What seems to be a course of action is for agriculture to utilize the contributions of each approach toward some kind of dialogical wholeness. This approach is highly complex, and no simple solutions are offered here as a gimmick; but the pattern of the future seems to point in the direction of agricultural groups recognizing the merits of all approaches and relating them in the matrix of the total economy. When agricultural groups find their intersecting interests and can spell them out articulately and clearly, their essential story can be received by society at large and by political and social leaders, whose interest it is to listen and to work for an adequate economic return for agriculture.

A Word from Scientists

In May 1963 the Population Reference Bureau, Inc.,

in Washington, D. C. (an agency of biologists, sociologists, and economists founded in 1929 to provide and interpret facts and relate them to world affairs), published an informative report on "The American Farmer." The report closes in this manner: "The farmer's contribution to his nation remains momentous—and absolutely necessary. A healthy well-educated and prosperous farm population is essential to the future welfare of this nation."

4
Development
of Communities
and Congregations

It is in the nature of man to build, tear down, and build anew. This process is continuous in all parts of a living society.

Our culture makes fertile ground for change. Ideas and knowledge, machinery and technology, communication and transportation systems, commerce and credit are some of the resources available to town and country and urban people alike. Changes come about when individuals and groups use resources that have come within reach. The doors of change hinge on the decisions that people make in their daily lives.

Town and country communities are being influenced by economic and social changes in many ways. Some communities with a relatively stable population are undergoing improvement in quality. Others with a stable population are deteriorating. Some with a declining population are improving or holding their own. Yet this is not true for all of them. Some communities with growing populations are improving, others are deteriorating or have considerable deterioration.

Both deterioration and development are present in all communities, whether urban or nonmetropolitan. Through responsible citizens and groups the task of community development is to identify deterioration and to bring about development in its place. Some factors that may contribute to a deterioration of communities (and institutions) are outmigration, a reduction of the economic base, erosion of the human spirit, or a lack of encouragement from outside the community. Some factors that tend to encourage community improvement are inmigration, expansion of the economic base, a buildup of human aspirations, and appropriate encouragement from outside.

The disappearance of some small communities may help rather than harm individuals, families, and groupings of people. Consolidation of some institutions likewise may be beneficial. What is central, however, is not the consolidation of communities or institutions but the development of people. In keeping with such a value it may be that the continuance of certain hamlets and villages (or certain businesses, churches, or schools) is one of the most desirable things on the face of the earth. A bedrock feature of community and congregation development is the right and the need of people themselves to develop alternative courses of action and to make decisions appropriate to their situation.

Development of communities and institutions centers in human factors, not on blueprints or physical construction. Community development is concerned with persons in relationship, not merely with population growth.

What Constitutes Community Development

A fine publication on community development was written recently by a husband-wife team, William W. Biddle and Loureide J. Biddle. He has served as the director of community development, Institute of Strategic Studies, United Presbyterian Church, U. S. A. For several years she was supervisor of projects, Program for Community Dynamics, at Earlham College. Many definitions of community development, the Biddles point out, tend to deal with the tangibles that make easily written copy for newspaper columns. Community development, as they understand it, is a more difficult subject for the news media.

In *The Community Development Process* the Biddles define community development as "a social process by which human beings can become more competent to live with and to gain some control over local aspects of a frustrating and changing world." They continue, clarifying the meaning: "It is a group method for expediting personality growth, which can occur when geographic neighbors work together to serve their growing concept of the good of all. It involves cooperative study, group decisions, collective action, and joint evaluation that leads to continuing action. It calls for the utilization of all helping professions and agencies (from local to international), that can assist in problem solving. But personality growth through group responsibility for the local common good is the focus." [10]

Coolie Verner, professor of adult education at Florida State University, underscores the centrality of personal growth in community development when he says: "The process is of more importance than the results achieved. In other words, it is not the building of playgrounds that is of importance, but what happens within an individual's consciousness to mold him into an intelligent, participating member of a democratic society."

Verner discounts programs that parade as community development. He makes this charge: "Quite often professional leadership plans *for* the community rather than *with* it and the programs that result are called community development, when in reality they are poorly disguised institutional activities."

The wellsprings of community development are neither purely internal nor external to the geographic community in which it takes place. Community development finds its source in a view of man that seeks the development of persons in responsible relation to others. Neither the individual nor the group takes precedence over the other. Both develop through interaction. Nor are external parties necessarily inimical to it. As such, a specific community development process may be initiated from within or from without. When initiated from within, great caution needs to be exercised that partisan objectives do not abort the endeavor. When initiated by a party outside the community, it is essential that genuine human relationships be established over a course of time. Tendency toward self-interest of an outside group or institution defeats community development.

In addition to the central theme of personal-group growth, several elements of community development may be helpful to mention.

    1. It relates to a specific community defined by

the community participants.

2. It concerns itself chiefly with the way of proceeding, the means. The ends to be achieved are secondary, by-products. (By-products have appropriate value.)

3. It concentrates on basic goals and purposes common to citizens and groups of the community.

4. Being a creative process, it is not overly concerned with a timetable of performance. A willingness to use large spans of time is essential. It is not production oriented.

5. It develops a climate out of which leadership emerges.

Community development tailor-makes its functions of a size that is appropriate to the community. Bigness, a popular status dimension, is of no central concern. The Biddles speak of "microprocesses in the midst of macroprograms." They write: "The comprehensive solution to problems, well-financed, affecting the lives of great numbers of people, and administered from the top, represents a macroprogram. One of the bars to the progress of community development is the widespread belief that only in macroprograms there is hope."

Informality is one of the characteristics of community development. Decision making is not to be compressed into a tight agenda that is taken care of in a "well run" business meeting. A community developer's experiment illustrates the point. In a certain county two groups of similar size (about 10) and composition were assembled to explore an identical concern: the development of their county. One group had an agenda. The person having most familiarity with each subject, or the most forceful person, spoke to it. Some spoke to no subject whatsoever. Decisions were made in response to the agenda. The meeting concluded in about 50 minutes, and the participants left with little or no carry-over of informal conversation. No new approaches or ideas arose. Specific needs were referred to appropriate agencies or institutions. The other group was given no agenda but was asked merely to discuss the concern (in the form of a question). All participants exchanged views. Most spoke on many occasions as information and ideas were shared; two or three spoke only a few times. The meeting lasted about 2 hours. Some new ideas emerged. After the meeting the participants left in small clusters, continuing to discuss subjects that arose.

There is an essential difference between business meetings and the informal meetings required in community development. Persons who intend to be helpful in any development process need to be aware how easily a meeting can lose its people-centered character.

Theological Basis for Participation

Does Christian faith commit a person to interest and participation in community development? In response to a questionnaire preparatory for a mid-America workshop of churchmen in the fall of 1962 at Iowa State University, over 80 percent of approximately 300 church council members of Lutheran congregations in the seven-state area responded affirmatively. An observation made of this response was: "Perhaps this indicates that church people are not as pietistically aloof from social responsibilities as sometimes thought."

The Trinitarian faith is a view of life that brings the Christian into active participation with the world as one of its stewards. Luther's explanation to the First Article of the Apostles' Creed carries widely taught expressions regarding Creation. "I believe that God has created me and all that exists. . . . Therefore I surely ought to thank and praise, serve and obey Him." Catechetical expressions can help to open our thoughts to the world.

In brief, the world is composed of family, community, occupations, and the larger environment of the natural orders. As Christ reconciles the person to God in salvation, he has a new basis for a creative relationship with his family, community, occupational pursuits, and the world at large. God encompasses the world and all its functions. The Holy Ghost, the Third Person of the Trinity, companions man in his stewardship of the earth. "The doctrine of the Trinity," affirms T. Watson Street in the Preface to a book on the Trinity, "will save us from the error of denying God's work outside the Church and the opposite error of so identifying the dynamic movements of history with the work of God that the Church is judged almost solely by her involvement in those movements. The doctrine of the Trinity will teach us that the spheres of life are subject to Christ, not to the Church, and that Christ's Lordship over these spheres is manifested by his Spirit, working . . . through lay Christians in the institutions of political, economic, and cultural life." [11]

Two principles of Christian social action are discussed by Louis Almen in *The Silent Struggle for Mid-America*. First, the critical or essential principle is the Word of God for man. "When the church is truly the church fulfilling its function of proclaiming the Word of God, it also discharges a most valuable social responsibility." Life under judgment of God's Word is the critical function. "By a relevant and proper preaching of the law of God it [the church] prepares people—farmers, businessmen, community leaders, teachers, preachers, housewives—all of us—for change."

Second, the creative principle of Christian social action is the Christian person. Faith represents an open, positive attitude that is willing to venture. By its nature faith is creative. Faith is active in building and renewing human relationships. Through "faith active in love" the Christian is a co-worker with God providing for man and building community.

The church in its organized form ought not enter the realm of community development directly. Its function is to provide for worship and Christian instruction and to be a spiritual family equipping members for life and service. The church as institution has responsibility for the critical function and must fulfill this essential mission. The danger in the organized church taking part directly in community development is twofold; it may forsake the critical function, and it does encroach on the creative function.

On the other hand, the people of God in the world have the responsibility to participate in community development. The function of the church as people (not as organized church) is to pursue responsibilities as citizens in the public realm, relating to other people and institutions that apply to the situation. The strength of this approach to social action is twofold: it employs the gifts and capabilities of all men, and it is open to the guidance of God.

For clarity it may be said that the critical function represents the ministry of the Word of God performed by the pastor and congregation as the gathered people of God. The creative function represents the ministry of Christian faith performed by laymen as the people of God in the world. The primary setting for the pastor's ministry is in the church. For the layman's ministry it is the world. How well the pastor is able, in human terms, to unfold and apply the Word of God to community development is a test of his craftsmanship. How well the layman is able to share in the process of community development tests his creativity.

Here is a graphic portrayal of the church's role (through people) in community development.

	Critical Function	*Creative Function*
Centers in:	Word of God	Christian person
Relates to:	Worship and education of the church	Work and development of the public community
Takes lead in ministry:	The pastor	The laymen
Objective:	Christian growth	Community development

Congregations and denominations that have a church-type ministry find it proper to relate to community development. Congregations and denominations that have a sect-type ministry find it difficult. A framework of comparisons may help to identify the church's role in relation to community development.

Church-type Approach	*Sect-type Approach*
1. Administers the means of grace, charging the people of God to conduct themselves in a faithful ministry in and stewardship of the world.	1. Administers the means of grace and separates the elect from the nonelect. Suspicious of the world, even of its people in it.
2. Regards both the Christian community and the citizen community as within God's reign.	2. Thinks only the Christian community is within God's reign.

3. Preaches, believes, and seeks to live the Trinitarian faith.	3. Preaches and believes the Trinitarian faith but neglects Articles I and III of the Apostles' Creed.
4. Encourages both laymen and pastors to fulfill their respective citizenship duties.	4. Tends not to encourage laymen and pastors to fulfill citizenship duties.

Langdon Gilkey's new book, *Shantung Compound,* provides an interesting study of community. One of its points deals with human relationships. The fundamentalist and legalistic approach of some of the religious prisoners proved to be at the same time both quick to condemn and selfish. The result was a tendency to destroy community rather than build it.

Church Realignment as Development

No one knows how many consolidations or mergers of congregations have taken place since the settlement of the American countryside. But it is certain the number is very high. Church realignments have taken place within denominations, both Catholic and Protestant, to adjust to a larger scale of social and economic life which accompanied the shift from 19th- to 20th-century technologies in agriculture, communication, and transportation.

Many laymen, pastors, and church administrators acknowledge that the greater number of church realignments are likely yet to come. Inducements from technological change are being reinforced by much closer harmony fostered within and among denominations by the ecumenical movement.

Several guidelines may be helpful when facing situations where church realignment seems desirable. First, the approach needs to be guided by the Christian doctrine of the church. Second, church alignment deals with form or structure as means, not ends. Here, too, form is to follow content; structure is determined by purpose. Third, church realignment must be grounded in the Christian growth of individuals and of the community of believers. It is the result of a developmental process. Fourth, there are no shortcuts in church realignment. Congregations forced together for one reason or another do not merge authentically. Last, church alignments grow best from within. This is to take seriously the Christian doctrine of man.

Church realignment never belongs in the forefront. It is a corollary, a by-product, of the church's mission. How a congregation or a group of congregations structures for mission is centered in the mission for the particular situation. Church realignment or consolidation of congregations is most appropriately a people-centered process of development. It might be referred to as congregation development.

Sometimes church agency personnel or pastors hurry to suggest or recommend consolidation or realignment. This is easy to do without recognizing the essential process of personal and group growth. Then such well-meaning suggestions may only delay congregation development.

A certain pastor in the Midwest once estranged himself from two of the three congregations in the parish he was serving. "Why don't you close these two country congregations and merge with the larger one in town?" he suggested. His question marked the beginning of a decline in his relationship with both congregations. They resented his suggestion.

When he accepted a call to a two-point parish in another area, he vowed he would serve St. James, 7 miles from town, and Redeemer, in town, to the best of his ability and himself never bring up the matter of consolidation.

After a church council meeting at St. James, nearly 3 years later, laymen themselves raised the issue. As the pastor was getting into his car, several of the men approached, and one of them began: "Say, Pastor. We've been wondering, been talking among ourselves. Could we meet with the church council of Redeemer on the possibility of getting together?" They brought it up, not he.

An invitation was extended by Redeemer for exploration, study, and discussion. It was not long before the two congregations became one. When the people of the congregations studied and discussed their situation, they grew together. On the basis of what they learned about their situation, one another, and their common mission, it was decided they could do better as one congregation.

After the issue was raised by the people, the pastor could speak to it. Nevertheless his role was to encourage communication and to help find appropriate ways to open and keep open the avenues of communication. He acted in his pastoral role and did not seek to administer what was a people-centered process of development.

Congregation development is a twin of community development. Whenever the end becomes more important than the means, development is short-circuited. Community development literature can be helpful to laymen, pastors, and administrators who have concern for congregation development.

Congregation development and community development are interwoven through people. As persons take part in either process, growth occurs in relation to basic values, to other persons, and to groups. Following a congregation development experience in one of the Great Lakes states (which resulted in a consolidation of three congregations into one) members in their creative function as citizens became meaningfully involved in community development. Congregation development increases the ability of individuals for public responsibilities.

Community Development in the Larger Context

"We have an opportunity to bring closer together all parts of our population, our economy, and our geography and so to help us realize that the prosperity of city people is tied closely to the well-being of rural people, that many traditional distinctions between city and country no longer are true, and that the United States is one Nation, indivisible." These are the words of Secretary of Agriculture Orville L. Freeman in his Foreword to *A Place to Live: The Yearbook of Agriculture 1963.*

In the same volume editor Alfred Stefferud writes: "City and country people have a stake in the maintenance of healthy conditions in country and city. Because a progressive, viable rural economy and the full use of its resources benefit the entire Nation, we stress the unity of our interests. What kind of rural America do we want, and how do we get it? What changes are needed in attitudes about resources? How must Federal, State, and local governments work with people to develop programs that will meet our goals for improved living and working conditions? What are our goals, values, objectives?"

Questions of this quality were raised in New Jersey in its effort to conserve farms and open space as referred to in Chapter 1. Major social questions have a significant way of encouraging major social responses. Questions open doors to dialog and interaction. Asking and listening pave the way for communication that is more than monolog.

Boards and commissions of many nonmetropolitan counties are hiring consultative or planning services. Architects and planners are engaged to make inventories and projections. Town and country counties and communities are wise to seek the counsel and services of professional groups to assist local efforts. Among important actions for community development groups are those of keeping a current inventory of needs and potentials and of developing relationships with public and private resources at both state and national levels.

The emergence of county and multicounty planning agencies in town and country is a constructive factor in assisting people to develop their communities, human potentials, economic base, and natural resources. Community development groups find county and multicounty planning units to be a force helping to shape the future. Persons who staff planning units want to relate to the aspirations and values of people.

State economic development agencies provide a wide variety of service to communities and counties that seek to develop themselves. Community leaders do well to establish a relationship with their state's economic development agency. These agencies have a keen interest in helping to meet local needs. They have staff specialists who serve as resource persons for particular needs of local groups. We tend to be less familiar with state agencies than good judgment would suggest.

Federal Programs for Individual and Community Advancement is a resource pamphlet of the Office of Information, U. S. Department of Agriculture (Agriculture Handbook No. 312). The pamphlet describes programs in 25 classifications. Community development is fourth on the list. Programs under it are:

- Appalachian Regional Commission

- U. S. Department of Agriculture
    Agricultural Stabilization and Conservation
        Service
    Farmers Home Administration
    Rural Areas Development
    Soil Conservation
- Department of Commerce
    Economic Development Administration

- Department of Defense
    Army Corps of Engineers
- Department of Health, Education, and Welfare
    Welfare Administration
- Department of Housing and Urban Development
    Community Facilities Administration
    Urban Renewal Administration
- Office of Economic Opportunity
    Community Action
    Volunteers in Service to America (VISTA)
- Small Business Administration

Community development seeks to relate to larger units of society. It does not isolate itself from colleges and universities, service organizations, private foundations, state and national governments. It recognizes that such groups can further the aims of local groups. Town and country communities sometimes place an inflated value on independence. Familiarity with resource agencies can lead to a discovery of interdependence and constructive interaction.

Wisdom, Sensitivity, and Joy Build Community

If we seek a society that has greatness, it is necessary to know and develop the qualities of greatness. Biographies of great persons yield some insights regarding these qualities. Wisdom is one: being wise is to harness potentialities for human enrichment. Helen Keller and those around her grasped and utilized many possibilities for human enrichment. What they have done reaches far beyond their immediate circle. Sensitivity is another: being open to the expressions and feelings in nature and among persons. Augustine teaches us to be open to the world and its creatures. A comment of Lincoln reflects sensitivity to persons: "I don't care for that person; I must get to know him better." Joy is another, in the sense of Nehemiah 8:10: "The joy of the Lord is your strength." Notable in recollections about Dietrich Bonhoeffer is this reflection of joy by a fellow prisoner: "Bonhoeffer . . . always seemed to me to diffuse an atmosphere of happiness, of joy in every smallest event in life. He was one of the very few men that I have ever met to whom his God was real and close to him."

Wisdom, sensitivity, and joy, each in a deep human and theological sense, are some marks mirrored in the lives of great men and women. Where citizens and leaders possess these traits or are possessed by them, some of the basic ingredients for community development are present. It is encouraging to encounter persons of such persuasion in small towns and large cities; on farms and ranches; in industrial plants and hospitals; among salesmen and scientists; in local, state, and federal government offices; in schools, colleges, and universities.

Great persons are present in cities and in the countryside, in all the diverse settings of American life. Their persons and energies exert a social force toward the development of the human community across the land.

5 Human Relations in Town and Country

Human relations has to do with what we think of other people, how we speak of them and with them, how we act toward them. As in the case of community development, human relations recognizes and appreciates the humanity, worth, and capabilities of other persons; seeks to know other persons and to be known by them; and enjoys life in the presence of others. Donald H. Larsen of the Lutheran Council in the U. S. A. says human relations is the "art of encounter as humans without regard to race, creed, national origin, or social class or caste."

Many men and women in town and country have a commitment to human relations. They have a conviction that much needs to be done to improve the understanding of people and communities regarding "other" people. Some seemingly have no opinion or express no particular conviction. Some resent any mention of the subject and of finding ways to help relate to various people in our diverse society.

Human relations in town and country begins with the birth of our nation, has present dimensions of breadth and depth, and has a future that holds promise. The need is not confined to the cities.

In all events of change, wisdom calls for openness of mind and heart, a willingness to understand what is happening in society and why, and the readiness to help develop constructive approaches. Wisdom calls for reexamination of one's own experiences, attitudes, and values.

Harry Golden once said: "I read it somewhere in the Hebrew writings: When a man fights for others he really fights for himself."

Christians have a recollection from one of the New Testament letters that frames responsibility in this way: Share the burdens of other people, for this is what Christ wants His people to do.

Participation in Mass Society

The small town is inextricably a part of mass society. This is a major point of the careful study on *Small Town in Mass Society* by Arthur Vidich and Joseph Bensman. In 1960 Lowry Nelson wrote his analysis of *The Minnesota Community, Country and Town in Transition*. He focuses attention on people and communities of the countryside but affirms that they must be seen "in the context of the Great Society."

Early in his systematic inquiry of one of our major urban centers (Detroit) Gerhard Lenski refers to the "steady decline of localism and regionalism in America." The interaction of urban and town and country persons is also identified by Paul Price and George Hillery, Jr., in their discussion of *The Rural-Urban Fringe and Louisiana's Agriculture*. In their study they found "an intermingling of rural and urban people, ideas, values, and philosophies."

Town and country communities share in the life of the nation — its needs, potentials, problems, and solutions. Through the interrelations of urban and town and country people the substance of beliefs and values becomes common to both. Social needs and responses belong simultaneously to town and country people and to those in the cities. Concepts of city and rural residents alike have roots in past generations. Lenski states: "At the very least [these concepts] reflect the exposure of past generations . . . to the social environment of earlier eras."

In addition to direct contact by individuals and families through occupational, recreational, and residential factors, mass media contribute to the interrelatedness of urban and town and country people. R. D. McKenzie in his book, *The Metropolitan Community*, written before the advent of television, theorizes that mass communication is "responsible for merging traditionally distinct rural and urban cultures."

How Small Towns Hinder or Help

A sketch of two families illustrates how town and country people, congregations, and communities are related to issues in a diverse society. The members of the two families indicate how individuals either hinder or help in human relations according to values learned in the home, church, and community during formative years.

Both families are based in small towns and have extensions into urban centers through the outmigration of youth. Both families are active in the church. All children involved received the means of grace and Christian instruction, are graduated from local schools, leave home, and establish themselves in new settings.

Family A lives in one of the Great Lakes states. It is a fine family. The parents are respected citizens. The children make records in school that any parent could be proud of. At no time did they ever encounter the "race question" in a serious way in their home, congregation, or community.

The daughter goes to college, meets and marries an upcoming executive of similar background. They make their home in an apartment near the downtown area of the city where his company's main offices are. They join a downtown church that "serves the entire city." When the congregation begins to serve people of other economic and racial groups, now moving into the vicinity of the church, the couple simply and quietly withdraws and joins another congregation "where there are no integration problems."

The older son becomes an electrical engineer, moves where a job offer invites him. He establishes his home in "a community that will not have to worry about the race issue for a long time." He keeps his "nose clean," lives in affluence, and contributes little of his natural gifts to work with people. When the congregation he belongs to invites members to sign a public open-housing statement voluntarily, he chooses not to. "Why stir up trouble?" he reasons. "Things are quite peaceful in town now."

The younger son becomes a landscape architect and

joins a summer-home resort developer. In the private association only "qualified" families can buy lots and build. Once he overheard a salesman assure a prospective buyer: "You can be sure only people like yourselves will be able to buy property at Haven Lake Resorts." The younger son knew this meant no Indians, Orientals, or Negroes. It bothered him a little, but then, "there must be other places for them."

It never occurred to Family A, its congregation and community, that it was somehow related to the race question. The parents could be recalled to have said, "We have no race problem here." Church organizations discussed other races only in relation to "foreign missions." Never did any of the successive pastors show any particular concern for race issues. In the case of Family A three persons came within ministering and witnessing distance of the "race problem." But each turned away.

Family B lives in a community on the Great Plains. In most respects it is much like Family A. There are two children, a daughter and a son.

During a series of sermons dealing with Christian response in social concerns, Family B became embroiled in a tension that can be healthy for a congregation. Pastor Varmlund said from the pulpit: "Yes, Norwegians, Germans, and Swedes are our responsibility. And God loves others as much as He loves us. They are Indians and Mexican migrant workers, Negroes and Orientals. If some of these people move to our town, I trust you would befriend them, welcome them to town and to church.

"Some of you will be taking up work and residence in other areas of the country," he said, "especially you young people. I trust you will see people of other ethnic and racial groups as our Lord sees them — as brothers and as children of God."

Several members couldn't wait to tell the pastor a thing or two after the service was over. "Now look, Pastor, you can't be preaching that kind of stuff." The comments grew worse.

At the next church council meeting the issue was opened up again. Some men, among them the husband and father in Family B, agreed with Pastor Varmlund's approach and gave him credit for "sticking to his guns." A way through the conflict of ideas was found. The experience became the occasion for many in the congregation and others in the community to examine their own ideas and opinions. It sharpened the realization of the children in Family B as to what their parents believe and what the church teaches.

The daughter of Family B became a registered nurse, married a career military man, and since has lived in many communities. She is serving in a hospital in the East now. She has worked in five different hospitals, caring for people of every description and circumstance. When an elderly Negro lady tells her gratefully, "You're okay, honey!" her cup of reward runs over. In the Sunday school class she teaches are children of three racial groups. How alike they are to the children in the congregation of her childhood and youth. She and her husband and their children share friendships with families of the three racial groups. How good it is, she has reflected, to have been prepared at home and in church to live life in a diverse society!

The son of Family B becomes a soil conservationist, serving one of the more than 2,900 soil and water conservation districts in the United States. At a meeting of the district's board of directors he announces that a new trainee-assistant is a Negro who plans a career in soil science. He reports that Aaron Smithson will arrive in a couple of months and says: "I don't know how you men feel about race. But as for me, I want to tell you, I'm color-blind. Aaron and I will be traveling through the county together to get acquainted with people and the work. After that he will be calling on cooperators, carrying out the work. I will back him to the hilt. The way you men regard this is of real interest to me and, I think, will reflect the way he will be received. What's your reaction?"

There was no pause. One of the directors came in immediately: "That's the way we like to hear you talk. Power to you. We need every man who'll work with us. If it's Aaron, it's Aaron. I say welcome to him." There was spontaneous general accord.

What families and congregations in town and country think or do not think, say or do not say, and do or do not do in relation to social issues and needs has a direct bearing on many circumstances. Learning social values in early years influences actions later in life. Small towns—their people and institutions—either hinder or help human relations. Perhaps it may be more accurate to state that all small towns have both constructive and negative influences in race relations. What is needed is to find ways to increase the constructive factors.

A Survey of Ministry to Minority Groups

In 1962 Lawrence W. Halvorson, then secretary for human relations of the National Lutheran Council, prepared a questionnaire to be sent to Lutheran pastors in preparation for a multicounty workshop in town and country. The purpose was to discover how numerous were people of minority groups in the area and how aware of them the pastors were.

Forty-two questionnaires were sent out. Twenty were completed and returned. To one pastor the whole thing seemed useless. He wrote: "In the entire area the minority group problem ranks in importance to a wart on a calf's hide."

The first question asked: "What minority groups live in your county?" Responses indicated that the pastors generally were unaware that there were as many present as is revealed by Bureau of Census reports. Seven said they did not know. Six put down Indians. Three listed Mexicans. Chinese and Negro people were each cited on three different responses.

The second question asked: "How many Indians live in the area of the survey?" Eleven responses said there were none. Three ventured estimates of 300 Indians. The Bureau of Census report indicates that in 1960 there were 1,460 Indians in the area in over half of the 21 counties studied.

To a question concerning the ways congregations in the area minister to various minority groups there were five responses. Comments were made as follows: "There are a few Mexicans in Sunday school." "We try to provide jobs, hand-outs, food, and worship." Of the 20 responses to the questionnaire, one fourth indicated some approach to ministry. In other words, somewhat over 10 percent of the 42 congregations in the area indicated some ministry to minority groups.

The survey is regarded as reflecting general response by congregations to minority groups in town and country. It helped some to recognize that minority groups are present when they seem not to be and that human relations is a proper concern in town and country.

In the summary of the survey Pastor Halvorson states: "We are much too unaware of the diversity of people living in the counties where we live. We have been ministering to people of our own groups almost exclusively. But our eyes need to be opened to see all people that live within serving distance of our congregations and churches. Our concern is to emphasize humanity in our diverse society and to underscore the church's responsibility of having truly Christian concern for all people. Every congregation needs to realize that it is responsible for the people in its surrounding area. Whoever they are, they are of eternal worth in God's sight."

The 1960 Bureau of Census report for the multi-county area shows 1,460 Indians, 155 Negroes, 21 Chinese, 183 Japanese, 14 Filipino, and 31 others; total: 1,864. People of minority groups live and work in town and country. For too long, it seems, we have had the impression that they were not present or present only in such numbers as to be of minor significance. Is any single person or group of persons of minor significance?

Openness to Newcomers Needed

For most communities in the United States "newcomers" are on the increase. It is said that about 20 percent of our population moves each year. It would be hard to find a city that is not made up largely of "newcomers." It would be equally difficult to find very many town and country communities that do not have many "newcomers." We are a nation of "newcomers."

The term newcomer means different things to different people. In some communities it means a person or family that has come during the previous few months or year and perhaps not more than two years ago. In other communities it may mean a person or family of the most recent arrival, even though they may be the second generation in that community. A pastor in a certain town and country area once said: "If one doesn't live here at least 10 years, he is thought of as a stranger just passing through."

More and more town and country communities are witnessing the growth of the rural nonfarm population.

While the strictly farm population is decreasing, rural nonfarm population is growing. Congregations need to be alert to new rural nonfarm residents. Too often they are overlooked, regarded as "strangers passing through," or neglected because they are "newcomers."

In preparation for the mid-America workshop referred to in Chapter 4, members of town and country committees of Lutheran districts and synods were asked to interview six rural nonfarm families with the aid of a brief questionnaire.

Rural nonfarm people, on learning of the purpose of the interviews, responded favorably and with considerable interest. It was found that rural nonfarm people are often overlooked, not served, by the churches. About half of those visited were not served by any congregation.

One interviewer found four families who had moved into the community 8, 7, 4, and 2 years previously. Yet each reported that at no time had any layman or pastor of any denomination called on them to welcome them to the community or invite them to worship or to church school. "What an eye-opener these interviews were to me," he exclaimed in his report. "We've been falling down when it comes to serving people who move into our area."

In a book published by the National Lutheran Council in 1962, *New Thousands in Town and Country*, Mervin G. Smith and John B. Mitchell speak of the developing rural nonfarm population: "The concentration of population in metropolitan areas will continue accompanied by a flow of people into rural areas—who want to live in the open country but are not interested in commercial farming. The distance these people can live from their place of employment will increase. A continually improving highway system will reduce the time required to drive to a job in the city."

While there is a centripetal force drawing people to central cities, there is also a centrifugal force scattering people to the green spaces and open country for residence and recreation. Congregations and denominations need to be mindful of both movements. In their mission concern, congregations and denominations do well to assess the extent of the centrifugal flow of the rural nonfarm population. People who leave the cities are newcomers to the countryside toward which the church, if it is to serve in the midst of change, needs to foster openness among people in both the congregations and the communities of town and country.

Constructive Approaches in Human Relations

Encouragement, information, creative thought, and assistance by jurisdictional leaders and church agencies are helpful toward constructive actions in town and country. Congregations in all settings of society need both the counsel and the support of other congregations and their church bodies. Articles and letters in jurisdictional papers by laymen, pastors, and church administrators can help. Sometimes the responsibilities of congregations in town and country get lost in comparison with the more visible responsibilities in the cities.

One of the perceptive communications that does not lose sight of the responsibilities of congregations in town and country is titled "Small Towns and the Race Problem." It appeared in the December 1963 issue of *The Central Observer* and was written by Dwight F. Putman, then president of the Central Pennsylvania Synod, Lutheran Church in America. He observes that town and country communities are often segregated by the fact that only one race settled them. In counsel to congregations the article suggests three approaches:

    1. Avoid condemnation of others.

2. Replace complacency with concern.
3. Make a positive witness on behalf of the full and abundant life for men of all races.

In October 1963 laymen and pastors met at Augustana College, Sioux Falls, South Dakota, to study and discuss "The Church's Concern for a Diverse Society in the Upper Midwest." One of the discussion groups summarized their findings that concur with Putman's observations and counsel.

1. Communities and congregations should prepare themselves for the opportunity of welcoming Negro families.
2. Pastors should identify themselves with community projects to improve human relationships.
3. The church should be concerned about housing legislation and city ordinances which refuse lodging and food to Negroes.
4. Congregations are encouraged to invite Negro speakers to become better acquainted with each one as a person as well as a speaker.
5. Congregations are encouraged to enlarge (their understanding of) their local community to a vision of our whole nation.

The Chicago City Missionary Society and the Lutheran Human Relations Association of America (LHRAA) are two of the organizations that encourage and facilitate the visits of city children of racial and ethnic minority groups to host families in town and country. The visits of Negro, Puerto Rican, Indian American, and Appalachian children are of 1 or 2 weeks' duration. During the summer of 1966 about 6,000 children took part in the LHRAA's Rural Summer Vacation Program.

An Indiana family that hosted two Chicago young-sters for such a visit reported: "Until now Chicago was only a 'big city' to us. But now we think of Chicago be-cause of two little girls who were with us for a short time and have now gone back there."

A parish worker in a congregation from which chil-dren had been selected to visit farm homes in Iowa said: "Farm families were able to bring a striking witness to their friends and neighbors in their own communities. By accepting these children as their own, they opened the way for others to reexamine their feelings in human rela-tions."

Another response indicates a sense of discovery: "It's wonderful to learn to know other nationalities and races. The most wonderful part is that it wasn't forced on any-one, but the farmers wanted to do it." [12]

Photographs and articles in church jurisdictional papers in several areas of the United States during the fall of 1966 suggest that "Friendly Town" and the Rural Summer Vacation Program are well received by many congregations and communities.

Speaking at the 1959 conference of the American Country Life Association, Roy Buck affirmed: "The American community needs a new sense of mission, a new destiny. Is there hope for the development of a way of life in the human community that will yield for each person, regardless of occupation or station, the fullest sense of self-fulfillment?" [13] Buck makes application of his point to community development.

The application bears on the social needs in a diverse society. People of every ethnic and racial group in the national community compose its human resource. To encourage and facilitate the contribution of individuals and families of every ethnic and racial group can enrich both local and national communities. Local communities and the larger society face the related issues of national mission and self-fulfillment that Buck raises.

Church groups and private citizens have often sponsored refugees to America from adverse conditions in other countries. Individuals and groups have come to the thought of developing some type of residence sponsorship for people of various ethnic and racial groups from ghetto situations. Families who have the desire and means to live elsewhere but have not been able to overcome obstacles themselves might welcome assistance by church and community organizations. Where this has been done, local communities and institutions have been strengthened. Through residence sponsorship, communities and congregations may have opportunities to assist families and to help develop constructive approaches in human relations.

Americans possess a great deal of knowledge about financial and scientific functions and problems. There is need for knowledge about people by people. Laymen and pastors who help plan continuing education events at the land-grant universities may request presentations by social scientists on human relations. Where this is done, authentic information about ethnic and racial characteristics and experience is a constructive factor and a learning experience of social relevance for pastors and laymen.

Human Relations and the Gospel

During noon lunch at a church in town and country conference of laymen and pastors a few years ago a county extension agent and a group of pastors were visiting with a farmer who happened to be a Negro. The discussion centered on methods of farming. When the farmer mentioned that he cultivates his crops with a team of mules, the county agent asked whether he could hire someone with a tractor to do it more efficiently. "I have had custom work done several times," replied the farmer. "But each time I've tried it the roots of too many plants were cut by the cultivators coming too close. I can't say if it was done on purpose. But I noticed that it didn't happen that way in their own fields. I've found I can do a better job with my mules."

The group around him was drawn into a moment of deep realization of the gap between mechanical efficiency and human failure.

At a pastors' retreat in Chicago in 1965 Joseph Sittler spoke of two gospels: "the gospel that claims God's blessing of the way things are—including the injustices—and of course His blessing of those in charge of perpetuating the status quo" and "the gospel that maintains God is present and active in the concrete valleys and asphalt jungles of the city, in both tenements and mansions, in slum ghettos as well as suburbs and the rural countryside.

"Such a gospel calls for its followers to repent their collective sin of treating people as if they were less than human. It urges them to do something about the evils in their midst—exploitation and persecution of certain racial, economic and religious groups; indifference to the poor, the prisoners, the outcasts of society. It demands a righting of wrongs."

The role of the Christian is to love as Christ loves. "To mend the broken" is the Christian's mission. In a book by that name Karl E. Lutze says: "Loving is indeed an art, and it takes study and practice. With the mind of Christ the Christian observes how Jesus identified with those whom He loved.

"Accordingly, the Christian learns to know personally the Negro, the Puerto Rican, the Latin American, the Indian American, the man from Appalachia. He looks at the life they live, the dwelling place they inhabit, the jobs they can get, the security they possess, the background they have inherited, the problems that burden them. He learns to know their needs, their fears, their liabilities, their lonesomeness, their frustrations, their hopes. It is then and only then that he can begin to love."

On September 22, 1966, the Chicago *Sun-Times* carried an editorial about "The Word in Mississippi." In response to heavy-handed intimidation and efforts to hold fast to old segregationist patterns a clergyman spoke out. "He condemned the savagery of white adults who harassed and beat Negro children trying to attend two schools that had been ordered integrated."

It was thought that his words and actions were courageous in the extreme and would bring a fierce dissent, outcry, and possible danger. "But the Grenada minister—the Rev. C. B. Burt, a Methodist—evoked a startling and heartening response. Nobody walked out on him. At his call more than half his congregation of 500 persons came before the altar to kneel and pray for forgiveness. Some were weeping. Perhaps they had been waiting for the word. Perhaps somebody had to speak the word for them before they would move. Perhaps the people are waiting in many places." [14]

6 Outdoor Recreation in the Countryside

Outdoor recreation imparts vigor to the American society. Pulses are quickened and thought processes sharpened on the ski mountain or ocean surf. Even spectators at summer or winter athletic events are stimulated mentally and physically—fresh air, the walk around the golf course, the climb up to the ski jump. Or take some milder forms of outdoor recreation—bird-watching, plant photography, rock hunting—these, too, require energy and thought but also return a good measure of mental and physical renewal.

Landscapes and waters, living plants and wildlife offer something for man's humanity. The soft geometric and the nongeometric patterns in nature stand in contrast to the hard geometric patterns of man's civilized world. Living colors and smells in nature are constantly in motion in contrast to the static colors and smells in man's culture. Nature is always in motion. It is in the constant process of re-creation, regeneration. Perhaps the factor that inspires and renews is life in the process of being created in myriad colors, forms, and sizes.

To discover "being" within the order of nature — "All flesh is grass" (Isaiah 40:6) — constitutes a basic perspective for man. Nature is a symbiotic community in which man can see himself. It provides a necessary perspective for viewing himself in relation to more than himself. To discover "being" in the framework of nature is to learn a fundamental aspect of the Biblical message regarding creation. Man exists not independent from nature but in alliance with it. As Stewart L. Udall puts it: "We are not outside nature, but of it."

The great arena for nature in motion is the countryside. The countryside is and has what man cannot build. This is why both urban and town and country residents have a common stewardship of the outdoor recreation resources in their respective states and on a national scale. Wherever nature in motion can be retained or reestablished in urban areas, it is a gain to be lauded. However, the primary setting for man's recreation in nature is of necessity the countryside.

Outdoor Recreation Growth and Resources

It is difficult for people in urban and in town and country areas to recognize the importance of outdoor recreation, why it is expanding so rapidly, and the critical nature of outdoor recreation resources in both the public and the private sectors of our economy. The difficulty of perceiving the significance of outdoor recreation in the life of the nation may be akin to that of seeing life whole in a complex agricultural-industrial economy. In his book *The Next America* Lyman Bryson compares man to a cricket on a large, flashing electric sign. He does not know its overall design, yet he clings to the part where he is even though it is hot and lively there.

As in the case of agriculture, industry, commerce, education, and other fields, outdoor recreation is a hot and lively subject. While the totality of any major subject area is evasive, it is necessary to work toward a comprehensive understanding of the subject.

Outdoor recreation expansion rests on the footings of technological development in both agriculture and industry. Mechanization and the sciences have generated a widespread release *from* excessive demand on time for work *to* time free for personal pursuits and avocations in both city and countryside.

Vacation trips, weekend outings, and overnight jaunts are frequent experiences of millions of families. The increase in outdoor recreation is woven into the fabric of American economic and social life. Our population, now near 200 million, is expected to reach 230 million by 1976 and approximately 350 million by the year 2000. The workweek has been reduced to 39 hours, and pressures exist toward reducing it further. While the average annual paid vacation is now about 2 weeks, social scientists say that by 1976 it may be increased by nearly one third. Per-capita disposable income, at a record high, continues to mount. The Hudson Institute research staff estimates that in the year 2000 we will have a 3-day workweek, 13-week vacations, and over 13 percent of the U. S.

population earning at least $40,000 a year.

The Outdoor Recreation Resources Review Commission (ORRRC) report, *Outdoor Recreation for America,* says: "Whatever the measuring rod — visits to Federal and State recreation areas, number of fishing license holders, number of outboard motors in use — it is clear that Americans are seeking the outdoors as never before. And this is only a foretaste of what is to come.

"Commission studies show that participation in outdoor recreation during each summer may well leap from the present 4.4 billion separate outdoor recreation 'activity occasions' — participation by an individual in a single recreation activity during a day — to 6.9 billion activity occasions by 1976. By the year 2000, this total could rise to over 12.4 billion occasions, an increase of 184 percent over participation in 1960.

"About 90 percent of all Americans participated in some form of outdoor recreation in the summer of 1960."

In view of the growing demands for outdoor recreation, ORRRC proposed a classification for outdoor recreation resources — a helpful framework for understanding the various functions of these resources.

Class   I — High-Density Recreation Areas

> Intensively used areas such as beaches and parks in or near large population centers.

Class II — General Outdoor Recreation Areas

> Settings as picnic grounds or ski slopes, involving less crowded use.

Class III — Natural Environment Areas

> Forest and open areas providing outdoor recreation in a natural setting in which other uses

such as lumbering or grazing may take place. This is the largest class in both public and private holdings.

Class IV — Unique Natural Areas

Several factors identify these areas: extraordinary natural wonder and scenic or scientific value.

Class V — Primitive Areas

Remote from population centers and existing in the natural undisturbed condition. Noteworthy for inspirational, esthetic, scientific, and cultural values.

Class VI — Historic and Cultural Sites

Places of historic and cultural significance from a local, regional, or national standpoint.

In thinking of the growing demand for outdoor recreation and of the ORRRC classifications for outdoor recreation resources it may be well to view the land resources of the United States. While only brief mention is possible in these paragraphs, the ORRRC report has numerous charts and graphs on land resources, as well as explanatory written material, to give the interested reader much helpful information. In the 48 contiguous states in the year 1960 land ownership was as follows:

Ownership of Land	Millions of Acres
County or municipal governments	17
State governments	80
Federal government	407
Indian groups	56
Nonfarm groups	222
Farmers and ranchers	1,120
Total	1,902

Private ownership of land in the 48 contiguous states in 1960 totaled 1,342 million acres. Land held by local, state, and federal units of government, together with the 56 million acres held by Indian groups, totaled 560 million acres. These figures indicate why demands cannot be met by public groups alone.

Opportunities Outdoor Recreation Presents

What does the growth of outdoor recreation mean to individuals and communities? For one thing it means new opportunities for the development of businesses, facilities, employment, and income-producing activity. Both urban and town and country individuals and families are investing in outdoor recreation facilities or in land with outdoor recreation potential. In *The Next Generation* Donald N. Michael reports: "Recreational technology will offer enormous opportunities for engineering imagination and entrepreneurship."

Farmers and ranchers throughout the United States are developing farm and ranch vacation facilities for individuals, families, and groups. In some areas it is already a big business; in others it is beginning to catch on. In one area of Nebraska farmers developed facilities at their farms for hunters—providing rooms, meals, and hunting grounds on a daily, weekly, or seasonal basis. While tensions existed between hunters and farmers in previous seasons—hunters failing to respect crops and fences and farmers refusing permission to hunt—with the closer relationship came the mutual discovery of persons. Hunting and farming were compatible when people involved learned to know and appreciate one another. In such arrangements hunters achieve quality recreation experiences, and the farmers strengthen their economic base.

The Crow Wing Trail in Minnesota is an example of local leaders developing an imaginative outdoor recreation facility. The idea was stimulated by the Land and People Conference of September 1963 in Duluth, where the late President John F. Kennedy spoke: "Our goal must be cooperative effort. It must coordinate the efforts of public agencies and private industries. It must apply the principle of multiple use to all the resources of this area."

To the Wadena Soil and Water Conservation District directors the Crow Wing River appeared to offer possibilities. A joint project was formed of five soil and water conservation districts and the boards and commissioners of five counties — Wadena, Swift, Pope, Kandiyohi, and Otter Tail. The project now totals about 3½ million acres (90 percent privately owned); 75 miles of scenic canoe trail; campsites from 10 to 22 acres in size, donated by a citizen, two industries, and county governments; a new Crow Wing Wilderness Saddle Trail; and 60 miles of Crow Wing snowmobile trail.

John Rife, chairman of the Crow Wing Canoe Trail executive committee, reports that many constructive experiences are intertwined in this first of 10 resource conservation and development pilot projects in the United States. "A father and son would take one day the first year, the next summer . . . the whole family. Boy Scouts, Girl Scouts, and church groups have frequently used the canoe trail since the beginning. Scouts have received merit badges in projects such as wildlife set up by the Canoe Trail committee. People like the freedom, the wilderness atmosphere, and the variety of bird and animal life. Each [of our projects has been] a dream of local people waiting for an opportunity to be realized. Those now in operation have provided 39 man-years of employment and increased local incomes an estimated $136,000 in 1965."

Educate for Outdoor Recreation

ORRRC concludes its report with this statement: "We urge all to push forward in a nationwide effort to secure the contribution that outdoor recreation can make to the well-being of the Nation and its people."

Education and research are basic approaches in bringing about the constructive influences of the outdoor environment. ORRRC says: "Perhaps no other activity involving so many people and so basic a part of our life has received less attention from qualified investigators and scientists." The newly formed Bureau of Outdoor Recreation in the U. S. Department of the Interior seeks to develop relationships with public and private education and research institutions to further knowledge about leisure time, the outdoor environment, and outdoor recreation. The approaches will relate to the sciences and humanities, to the liberal arts.

The Board of Education of the City of New York has begun a systematic program to study the city's outdoor environment. Parks, hills, valleys, plateaus, lakes, waterfronts, flood areas, swamps, springs, streams, eroded areas, unusual rock formations, excavations, buildings, places that sell building materials, schools, streets, fields, pavements, and the like provide the laboratories and lab supplies for classes in basic science. *Operation New York* is a publication that tells of this educational and research effort. It indicates that educators of a metropolitan area regard familiarity with nature as important in the life of urban citizens.

Scientific research at the academic and professional levels is the aim of the Bureau of Outdoor Recreation; however, opening avenues of concern and understanding is important at the elementary and high school levels.

When the Commission on the Humanities made its

report to the American Council of Learned Societies, the Council of Graduate Schools in the United States, and the United Chapters of Phi Beta Kappa, it dealt with the role of the humanities in rapidly growing leisure time. The report states: "A novel and serious challenge to Americans is posed by the remarkable increase in their leisure time. 'What shall I do with my spare time' all-too-quickly becomes the question 'Who am I? What shall I make of my life?' When men and women find nothing within themselves but emptiness they turn to trivial and narcotic amusements, and the society of which they are a part becomes socially delinquent and potentially unstable. The humanities are the immemorial answer to man's questioning and to his need for self-expression; they are uniquely equipped to fill the 'abyss of leisure.'" This report implies an enlarging role of liberal arts colleges in the American society.

Theological, ethical, and philosophical groups need to dialog, probe, study, and synthesize information and insights concerning the outdoor environment, leisure, and recreation. Such approaches are under way. Robert Lee of San Francisco Theological Seminary discusses the need for a leisure ethic in his helpful treatment of *Religion and Leisure in America.* A number of social and physical scientists, theologians, and churchmen have begun a group to study the relations of faith, man, and nature.

"Europe, which has even greater population densities, has much to teach us about building recreation into the environment," ORRRC tells us. "Holland is constructing a national network of bicycle trails. In Scandinavia, buses going from the city to the countryside have pegs on their sides on which people can hang their bicycles. We are spending billions for our new highways, but few of them being constructed or planned make any provision for safe walking and cycling. And many of the suburban developments surrounding our cities do not even have sidewalks, much less cycle paths."

Communities of varying sizes and settings—such as Pasadena, Calif., and Prairie du Chien, Wis.—are helping people enjoy outdoor recreation through bikeways. Bike trails along streams, around lakes, and along highways (well marked for directions to cyclists and to warn motorists) are being developed in many states. Bible camps with sufficient land and scenic areas may find that a bike trail can enhance their outdoor recreation program at a relatively small cost.

Ways to encourage outdoor recreation education are through audiovisuals, literature, and speakers from conservation and recreation groups; group visits to an arboretum with a professional naturalist along to explain animal and plant life in depth; study groups that discuss informative works on the outdoor environment.

Nature Ministers to Human Needs

Various speakers and writers suggest that man go to nature for what it offers. John Muir wrote: "Climb the mountains and get their good tidings. The winds will blow their own freshness into you and the storms their energy, while cares will drop off like autumn leaves."

Writing in the *Christian Scholar* in 1961, Paul E. Pruyser suggests: "The outside world and its sensory qualities is not only there in all its intricacy and splendor but has also healing powers, as every occupational therapist knows."

One of the beautification projects in metropolitan Washington, D. C., attests to the balm nature offers. *Time* magazine (Sept. 30, 1966) records Mrs. Lyndon B. Johnson's observation of school beautification in poorer districts. "'Broken windows cost the District of Columbia

$118,000 each year,' she says. 'I stood in front of a school one day and counted 26 broken windows on one side alone. But—and here is the magic—at the nine schools we have landscaped, the breakage has dropped to almost nothing.'"

At the national Seminar for Outdoor Recreation held in 1964 under the auspices of the Division of American Missions office for Church in Town and Country (National Lutheran Council) Alfred L. Edwards, deputy assistant secretary of the U. S. Department of Agriculture, put it this way: "The out-of-doors nourishes the spirit as nothing else can. We all need to partake of nature's wonders as they are found in the countryside. We need this today more than ever before. President Johnson recognized this need when he urged us to protect and improve our countryside." In the discussions that followed, the question why nature "nourishes the spirit" was opened and pursued to some extent. This subject needs to be opened and pursued on many occasions.

That the outdoors does nourish the human spirit is a widely acknowledged phenomenon. When the unique ministry of nature is cited, Christian faith rejoices. This is the joy of the psalmist who sang, "Bless the Lord, O my soul! . . . who hast stretched out the heavens like a tent . . . who makest the winds Thy messengers, fire and flame Thy ministers" (Psalm 104:1-4). Christian faith affirms through Biblical accounts, creeds, and liturgy that nature ministers to human needs.

In a discussion of *Mater et Magistra* Jaroslav Pelikan reminds us: "There is a deep intuition in the human spirit that man's life came from the earth and is nourished by the earth. No religion dares become so *spiritual* that it loses sight of this intuition. Indeed, both Judaism and Christianity have at their center the affirmation that the God who redeems man is the God of the earth. . . .

"When the message of the Church forgets this affirmation or supposes that everyone knows this, and that therefore it does not have to be preached, the Church loses its ability to address the deepest needs of the human spirit." (*Country Beautiful,* January 1962)

There is Biblical evidence for the claim of the ministry that occurs within nature; yet nature of itself does not purify the heart of man. No ministry ever does. Spiritual renewal is the work of God. Ministries that He calls into being are channels or vessels of grace. The source is God. Nature is not God but His creation, created to serve His purposes.

Helmut Thielicke in his study of creation, *Man in God's World,* tells the story of Goethe's *Faust.* Faust has wronged Margaret. Suffering pangs of conscience he cradles himself in nature since, to him, nature knows neither care nor guilt. Faust seeks in nature "the place where God will not meet him in person, where he feels embosomed in a sequence of events which knows no guilt and no moral values."

The Bible, Thielicke affirms, presents a totally different, a contrasting view of guilt and nature. Man, with Faust, tends to seek in nature an environment beyond good and evil. But the Bible knows man only in the context of good and evil, ascribing responsibility for good or evil to man. It is significant, Thielicke observes, that the Bible's "nature-intoxicated psalm" closes as it does: "Let sinners be consumed from the earth, and let the wicked be no more!" (Psalm 104:35). "Isn't that like cold water poured on all the joyful exultation in nature found in the preceding verses?" Thielicke asks. Why the sudden reversal?

> The reason lies precisely in the fact that the Psalmist views nature as a drama in which *God* is acting. . . . He realizes that in the presence of this God he is a sinner, that there is a dark spot

in this lovely garden of God's creation and that this dark spot is his own heart.

In any case, there is one thing the Psalmist could not have said. He could not have said what Goethe was saying: Studying nature and delighting in nature I become a pantheist and therefore I am beyond good and evil. No, what he is saying in these concluding words is just the opposite: Wherever I may be, in my work, my marriage, my dreams, or my love of nature, on mountain height or ocean strand, there I am in the presence of the Holy God.

All the sick, sin-stained, restless hearts, these dark spots that interrupt the stainless light of God's created world, are healed, forgiven, and brought to rest in him whom the Bible in a mysterious allusion calls "the fairest of the sons of men."

And all the crosses the church erects in the countryside, especially those on the heights of creation, the tops of the high mountains, are intended to be signs that there is one place in this world where sin has been atoned and peace is available, a place where the new sun of righteousness dawns upon a world of God in which guilt-burdened hearts and even the groaning and travailing creatures beyond the realm of humanity no longer need to be lonely spots of darkness in a world of light.

This is the Christian view of nature—and at the same time the Christian view of God's "beyondness." [15]

Aspects of the Church's Ministry

At the close of the national seminar on outdoor recreation, mentioned above, a pastor related his reaction on being invited to participate. "When my church body asked me to leave a busy parish program for 3 days to attend a meeting on recreation, frankly, I was angry. I came with a chip on my shoulder, with the intention of speaking a strong word of criticism on the last day for involving us in such a frivolous subject.

"Presentations by persons from government and universities, on outdoor recreation resources and development needs, I found informative. But this information could be read, I reasoned. When social aspects and implications were presented, interest grew. As the theological reflections were shared and dialog ensued, I found myself drawn into the concerns. During the seminar I began to see new implications of outdoor recreation for the congregation I serve, for the community and county in which I live. I looked at my shoulder and the chip was gone."

In local congregations or groups of congregations, laymen and pastors are discovering more of the implications of outdoor recreation for congregations in the city, suburb, and countryside. Congregations can help people recognize and appreciate the ministry of nature through the eyes of faith. Harold Belgum says the signs and symbols common in outdoor recreation and used so often in the Bible—water, earth, air, and fire—"may turn out to be the most meaningful religious symbols in scientific America. The reason is twofold: they are elemental and Biblical, and they are available to all people in city, suburb, and slum as well as on a prairie, mountain, or plateau."

The main base and thrust of the church's responsibility to outdoor recreationists does not lie in special ministries. Yet it is true that in many instances special ministries, in existence or to be formed, are both appropriate and necessary. The main base and thrust, however, lies in faithful service and thoughtful proclamation of the Christian message by existing congregations in both urban and town and country areas. The task is to equip people for their "exodus into the world."

Congregations in town and country have responsibility to provide services of worship, Christian education, and counsel (as appropriate) by laymen and pastors. Alert churchmanship finds ways to make these services available to all persons who come into the area. Spiritual needs of individuals and families that arise during outdoor recreation trips may or may not be generally known. An example illustrates needs that congregations and their pastors in town and country are called upon to meet.

A community in the Great Lakes region, population about 1,500, is the setting of a series of events that provide an example of ministry to recreationists. Nearby is a large inland lake with a tent and trailer park. In town is Peace Church. Late in the morning of a summer day a caller arrives at the pastor's study, a teen-age girl whose eyes are red and whose face reflects emotional strain.

"We're out at the lake," she says. "Ever since we left Lansing, our family has been bickering and fighting. We can't agree on anything. Argue about everything. This morning everyone—my two brothers, my father and mother, and I—got into it worse, swearing and hating. I couldn't take it anymore. So I just grabbed the car keys and left. They're probably worried sick about what I might do. I've been driving and driving and decided to come here."

She spoke about 40 minutes, in response to an occasional question from the listening pastor. At length, after her emotion subsided, he asked her what help she may want. She asked for prayer for her family and herself. They concluded by praying the Lord's Prayer.

"What now can you do?" the pastor asked.

"I want to go back and tell them what happened, where I've been, what I've told you."

The pastor agreed and suggested she tell them why she came to visit with him. She left composed and with a certainty of her plan.

The following Sunday she and her family were at the morning service of worship. Afterwards the father stepped close to the pastor and with a firm handshake said softly, "We can't tell you how much healing has come into our family through this experience. We thank you."

Instances such as this occur in the ministries of countless congregations. The befriending listener is oftentimes a layman, oftentimes a pastor. It illustrates what Warren W. Ost means when he says a great deal of the ministry to outdoor recreationists is meeting urban problems in rural areas. Spiritual needs of the family from Lansing were met. The ministry gladly given will not show in "statistical gains" for Peace Church. The family was even of a different denomination. But a common mission of Christians in urban and town and country areas does come into view.

7 Land and Water for the Nation

No person lives or functions beyond his dependence on land and water. Even airmen, astronauts, cosmonauts, and the crewmen of ocean (surface or submarine) vessels depend on the earth for physical sustenance.

Land offers man a base for agriculture, foundation for buildings, and space for movement. Relations of the farmer, timberman, or small-town citizen to land are obvious and unquestioned. Urbanites may tend to think themselves relatively independent from land, especially those who live in high-rise apartments supported by combinations of concrete and steel. Yet the foundations of their residence go deep into the earth, and they need land resources for food, water, and mobility as surely as any farmer or rancher. In town and country man's relation to the land is largely in the horizontal plane and is quite apparent. In metropolitan areas man's relation to the land is more in the vertical plane and is less obvious or visible.

Man needs water for both the internal and the external care of his body. Agriculture and industry cannot produce without it. One of the most hellish aspects of a bombed-out city is the absence of pure water. On the other hand, when water floods over the countryside and city, agriculture, commerce, industry, and all other functions of society are disrupted. Water management is essential to civilization.

Land and water are often regarded as two separate resources, but earth scientists and hydrologists tell us the two are interdependent parts of a whole. Land and water are related in mutually beneficial functions. But if either is maligned, the function of the other suffers. Polluted water infects the soil; eroded soils stagnate the waters.

Metropolitan and town and country residents share a common dependence on land and water. The management and wise use of land and water are components of one of our most important national issues. Land areas, river basins, and watersheds of the countryside and metropolitan areas will be used and managed wisely for all of society and for all of nature, or we and our children will witness the extraction of exceedingly heavy reparations.

Information About Land Resources

Land is a fixed quantity. There are about 32.9 billion acres of land in the world, of which about 3.5 billion, somewhat over 10 percent, are generally considered arable. The amount in crops each year is about 2.4 billion acres, or about 7.6 percent. Not all of the earth's land area favorable for agriculture is distributed evenly. Europe, the United States, and India have the principal concentrations of fertile land. Several large land areas have but a small percentage of arable land—Latin America 5 percent, Australia and Canada each about 4 percent. (*Man, Land and Food,* U. S. Department of Agriculture, 1963)

Of the 1.9 billion acres of land in our 48 contiguous states, about 600 million, or nearly one third, are favorable for crop production. About 460 million acres are used for crop production annually. In 1961 a Land and Water Policy Committee was formed in the U. S. Department of Agriculture to estimate land needs in the future. The demand for cropland in 1980 was projected to be 407 million acres. Projections are affected by many variables such as population, export demand, and crop and livestock development. Two other studies estimate larger requirements for cropland acreage by 1980. Resources for the Future estimates the needs to be 437 million acres, and the 1959 Senate Select Committee put it at 480 million acres (approximately the amount of cropland in use in 1950).[16]

Soil scientists tell us that the central tenet of land management is use according to capability. Considerable duplicity occurs in our land use. A great amount of land is used according to its inherent capacity, but this measure of stewardship is also widely ignored.

Two reasons why land management suffers at the expense of land waste are the lack of basic information and the view that regards national resources as inexhaustible. Only the so-called climatic portion of the land resource—rainfall, sunshine, air, and temperature—are relatively constant and self-renewing. Another facet of land, fertility and moisture, though exhaustible by use, may be replaced or renewed within economic and physical limitations. The basic soil material — living soil — can be (and often is) exhausted and generally is not renewable. Basic soil is lost to water and wind erosion, highways and roads, industrial and urban development, or mining operations. To some extent basic soil is renewable, but this process is so slow and costly that its significance pales to nothing in comparison with wise management of existing soil.

Land is a complex natural resource. Topography, climate, types of soil, and past use are among the factors that give complexity. The following classification developed by soil scientists provides an introduction for laymen toward understanding the capability of various soils.

Class I land is level or nearly level and has deep soils that do not easily erode. It holds moisture well but requires good management to keep it productive. Its capacity for food production is very broad.

Class II land has soils with gentle slope causing water to carry soil away unless careful conservation is applied. Its soils are relatively deep, and the limitations are few, though its capability is not as broad as for Class I.

Class III land has moderately sloping soils that are sandy or shallow and have either too little or too much water. Choice of crops and agricultural methods are more limited than on either Class I or Class II land. More stringent soil conservation practices are necessary.

Class IV land is severely limited as to the crops it can host. Some soils in this class are suitable for grasses and for fruit or ornamental trees. The slope is moderately steep.

Class V land has soils that prohibit normal cultivated crops. Soils in this class are nearly all level but are wet or stony or lie in a floodplain. This land is not given to erosion and may be used for pasture, recreation, watershed protection, or wildlife habitat.

Class VI land has some soils that can be used for common crops but only under intensive management. It is generally unsuited to cultivation. Soils in this class slope steeply. Uses parallel those of Class V. Improvements may make Class VI land suitable for pasture or range purposes.

Class VII land is unsuited for cultivation. Its soils slope very steeply. Even grazing or forestry require careful conservation practices. Some of its soils may be suited to woodland. Recreation, watershed protection, and wildlife habitat are more suitable uses.

Class VIII land with careful protection may be used for recreation, watershed protection, and wildlife habitat. Included in this class are badlands, barren areas, sandy beaches, mine tailings, river wash, and rock outcroppings. Very steep sloping is characteristic of Class VIII land.

The Soil Conservation Service, U. S. Department of Agriculture, has an office in most counties that can provide interested persons with information about the classes of land in the local county or soil and water conservation district. Each district is directed by a board of local citizens who with the technical assistance of a soil conservationist (of the Soil Conservation Service) help each cooperating farmer to develop a conservation farm plan according to land capability. Increasingly, soil and water

conservation districts are providing technical assistance also
for urban land uses.

Land Larceny We Perpetrate

In spite of increased publicity about our vanishing
land and polluted waters, many Americans regard the
conservation of natural resources largely accomplished.
In reality the outcome hangs in balance. The late President John F. Kennedy, in his Introduction to *The Quiet
Crisis* by Stewart L. Udall, wrote: "The race between education and erosion, between wisdom and waste, has not
run its course. Each generation must deal anew with . . .
the tendency to prefer short-run profits to long-run ne-
cessities. The nation's battle to preserve the common es-
tate is far from won."

Each year we are losing about 12,000 acres of sand
beaches along the Atlantic, Gulf, Pacific, and Great Lakes
coastlines. If you are one of the 50 million people who
visit the beaches each summer, your favorite beach may
be in jeopardy. When man builds on sand dunes or alters
them in other ways, chokes rivers with pollutants and
constructs dams that inhibit sand flow, obstructs littoral
drift with breakwaters, groins, and jetties without regard
to the consequences, he blocks natural processes that
rebuild beaches and releases beach-destroying forces.
Increasing recreation demand suggests that ways be
found to multiply, not waste, shoreline recreation resources. The present depletion of our beaches robs them
from both current and future generations for partial
goals now.

We are still losing valuable soil resources through
faulty agricultural practices. In the fall of 1966 a young
Illinois farmer plowed the farm he rented to prepare for
the planting of corn and soybeans in the spring of 1967.

What makes fall plowing highly inadvisable on this farm is that it is made up of Class III and IV land. Erosion by wind but particularily by water runoff will tear tons of topsoil from the hills and slopes of the farm, carrying silt and soil into drainage ditches, waterways, and streams. (The Soil Conservation Service estimates that one inch of topsoil blown or washed from one acre amounts to 162 tons.) Despite clear advice of the soil conservationist to the contrary, the farmer persists in his ambition to farm corn and soybeans on land ill suited for them. Under such misuse the fertility of this farm will soon be lost. Hay crops that hold soil are suitable to the farm and are marketable. But hay farming has not as much prestige as corn and soybeans.

The number of farms that are still being farmed under the frontier philosophy and practice—deplete the soil and then move on—is appalling. The U. S. Department of Agriculture estimates that we are losing about 400,000 acres of good land each year to erosion and soil pollution. An additional 30 million acres of U. S. farmland has recently been pressed into production to meet rising world food needs, without careful management according to capability. Theodore Roosevelt once said: "To skin and exhaust the land will result in undermining the days of our children."

The adoption and management of conservation farm plans throughout the United States is a major accomplishment of recent decades. But this does not imply that the conservation job is done. Rather it marks the establishment of a federal, state, and local partnership for conservation.

Highways and roads consume enormous amounts of land each year. Land that goes into highways is a permanent loss from agriculture, recreation, and nature areas. As the space squeeze is under way, highways have become wider. It is estimated that at the time of the Federal-Aid Highway Act of 1956 about 15 million acres of land were in rights-of-way. The act called for an additional 2.5 million acres for building, widening, and relocating highways. The need for adequate highways is obvious; yet highway engineers and powerful state highway departments have the persistent tendency to claim the easiest routes. When this happens, prime agricultural land, streams, and natural areas (such as California redwood forest) are generally in jeopardy and often fall victim to the bulldozer.

Rapid population growth in the United States is being accommodated by rapid urbanization, particularly suburbanization. Unplanned or underplanned suburban sprawl brings developers leapfrogging into agricultural land. It is estimated that 1.5 million acres of farmland are being claimed each year by urbanization. This represents a 50-percent increase over 10 years ago. The enormity of annual loss and its swelling size cause a growing number of people to fear that we may sooner or later run out of good farmland.

Consequences of building factories and subdivisions on prime food-producing land are being felt, for example, in California. Crowding urbanization has forced fruitgrowers from the Santa Clara Valley to poorer land. Production costs are higher. Fruit quality is poorer. At this rate we may develop a country of beautiful houses and bad apples. By careful use of land according to its capability we could have both beautiful houses and good apples.

Mining operations have been and are notorious land spoilers. While some reclamation is practiced now, devastation in the multi-state region of Appalachia is one of the sorriest legacies of American industry. Nor is the federal government uninvolved. In his recent book, *A Wil-*

derness Bill of Rights, William O. Douglas states: "The federal government is heavily implicated in strip mining. TVA uses it (strip mined coal) extensively in its standby steam plants; and it owns extensive acres of strip mining mountains not yet touched. Why need our beauty feed those hot furnaces when other sources of power are so abundant?"

Two spokesmen for rational land use, one a soil scientist and geographer and the other an architect, speak prophetically about land waste. In *The Squeeze* Edward Higbee writes: "At the very time we are multiplying most rapidly, we have hit upon the most space-clogging form of community life." In *The Heart of Our Cities* Victor Gruen warns: "As long as we engage in land waste, our cities must waste away."

Information About Water Resources

Three fourths of the earth's surface is covered with water, and water is interlaced in the land structures of the continents. The endless circulation of water from the ocean to the land and back to the ocean is called the hydrologic cycle. While in its overall scheme it is simple enough, it is exceedingly complex in the functions of its many components.

In comparison with other countries the United States is supplied with excellent water resources. According to the U. S. Weather Bureau an annual average of about 30 inches of water falls as rain or snow on the 48 contiguous states. This amounts to nearly 5 million acre-feet or nearly 4.5 billion gallons per day (bgd). About 70 percent of this evaporates from the land and water surfaces, leaving about 30 percent for man's use. Of this amount we are presently using about one fourth. The rest flows back to the oceans.

The basic unit for water management is the watershed. A watershed is any area of not more than 250,000 acres (a statutory limit) that can be related to as a unit for flood prevention and water management. The value of watershed projects was demonstrated by the Flood Control Acts of 1936 and 1944 and also by the watershed program of 1953.

Present watershed projects are developed under the Watershed Protection and Flood Prevention Act of 1954 (Public Law 566). It provides for soil conservation districts, watershed districts, counties, municipalities, other local organizations, or the states to obtain federal technical and financial assistance for small watershed projects, flood prevention, and related water management practices. As of September 1964 the Secretary of Agriculture received applications for assistance for about 2,200 watershed projects. For the Soil and Water Conservation Needs Inventory (CNI) of 1965 a total of 12,781 watersheds were delineated in the United States.

Larger units for water management and development are river basins and major drainage areas. CNI mentions 160 principal river basins. In 1963 the Soil Conservation Service produced a benchmark study of this larger hydrologic unit, the *Atlas of River Basins in the United States*.

For overall water management purposes river basins are combined into 18 major drainage areas. In the eastern mainland are eight: New England, Middle Atlantic, Gulf and South Atlantic, Tennessee Valley, Ohio Basin, Great Lakes-St. Lawrence, Upper Mississippi, and Lower Mississippi. The remaining 10 lie in the western mainland: Arkansas-White-Red, Souris-Red, Rio Grande and Gulf, Missouri Basin, Columbia Basin, North Pacific, Great Basin, Central Valley, Colorado Basin, and Central and South Pacific.

Far more abundant than surface water is groundwater, another basic water resource. Groundwater is commonly regarded as all water that is in the ground. C. L. McGuinness of the U. S. Geological Survey defines groundwater as "the water under hydrostatic pressure in the pores and crevices of the rocks that is free to move under the influence of gravity from places where it enters the zone of saturation to places where it is discharged. It is a phase of the hydrologic cycle, and that fact is what both makes it a valuable, renewable resource and creates many of the difficulties that attend its full utilization. . . . It is in motion almost everywhere." [17]

The study by McGuinness employs 10 large groundwater regions. Each has geologic, physiographic, and climatic conditions that permit useful generalizations. The regions are Western Mountain Ranges, Alluvial Basins, Columbia Lava Plateau, Colorado Plateaus and Wyoming Basin, High Plains, Unglaciated Central region, Glaciated Central region, Unglaciated Appalachian region, Glaciated Appalachian region, and Atlantic and Gulf Coastal Plain.

Only brief mention of groundwater is possible in this essay. It is important that responsible citizens develop a reasonable familarity with groundwater as well as surface water. Public policy, or the provisions for wise long-range resource use, depends on the public being informed. Groundwater is playing an ever increasing role on the local, regional, and national scale. McGuinness reports our expanding use of this resource: "Groundwater pumpage in the Nation increased from something between 20 and 25 billion gallons per day in 1945 to 30 bgd or somewhat more in 1950 and about 47 bgd in 1960."

How We Desecrate Our Waters

Water resources are maligned by every conceivable unit of our society. Fortunately most units are beginning to recognize this and to take corrective action. But large questions remain. Are we ready to take adequate conservation action? Will the public support expensive antipollution measures? Are we too late?

The U. S. Department of Health, Education, and Welfare has publicized much information regarding water pollution. Here are some examples. Of New York City's 575 miles of waterfront, in 1963 only 35 were still safe for swimming. The Great Lakes are being polluted more quickly than special efforts can clean them. The Great Salt Lake in Utah receives 35 million gallons of raw sewage a day, not counting industrial wastes. Millions of dollars have been spent to clean up the Potomac River, but raw and partially treated sewage still runs in it alongside our national capital.

Water is being polluted in both metropolitan and town and country areas by establishments of the federal government. Into Chicago's frontal waters the U. S. Navy pours raw or partially treated sewage from its ships that stop by. The chief sanitary engineer of the North Dakota State Health Department describes the sewage facilities of the Minot Air Force Base as "only about half adequate." From its small lagoon smelly effluent proceeds into the countryside to the detriment of people, farms, and wildlife. Examples raise questions about other federal government practices and installations.

Our communities, urban and rural alike, are guilty of gross acts of water pollution. Storm and sewage drains run together in many cities flushing into lakes and streams that have lost the capacity to purify huge quantities of effluent. Small towns and larger trading centers in the countryside discharge their sewage into our waters after only primary treatment or none at all.

Industries are polluting waters in both metropolitan and town and country areas. One of the new creations of the metropolis is Indiana Harbor on Lake Michigan. One writer describes it as "rubble, petroleum wastes, and black organic ooze." Radioactive waste is a recent addition in water pollution. It comes from atomic reactors, uranium milling, medical laboratories, mortuaries, hospitals, and industries that use atomic processes and enters our surface and underground waters.

Nor does agriculture have clean hands in relation to water care. The Environment Pollution Panel of the President's Science Advisory Committee cites an example: "The excreta of farm animals are a major source of water pollution, entering streams, rivers or lakes either in surface runoff or through underground seepage, and posing hazards to human and animal health from pathogens common to animals and man."

Nature's Subsidy and Man's Responsibility

For centuries man steadily has increased his ability to extract and utilize the earth's resources. Agricultural and industrial wastes have been discharged for nature to cope with. In general nature has been able to assimilate these wastes. In some instances, animal manures for example, the effect has been positive barring overconcentrations.

But the industrial and technological revolutions coupled with the worldwide population explosion and the accompanying increase of crop and livestock production have altered radically nature's ability to break down and absorb mass effluent and wastes. Nature's capacity to purify air, water, and soil is enormous, but it has limits, as we are coming to discover. Mass society produces mass effluent and waste. As mass society foists these upon nature, it is extracting a heavy subsidy from nature. And subsidies usually have inherent limits.

Instances abound where nature's subsidies are being rapidly spent, have played out, or are already in deficit.

Watersheds and river basins of China have been denuded of their cover and forests so that once valuable mountain areas are now wastelands and the rivers are choked with sedimentation. Alpine forests were reduced to feed the timber needs of the once rich Roman Empire, causing Alpine pastures and meadows to wash away. Plant life and trees have been removed from California hillsides by fires and housing developments. Heavy rains then mire stylish homes and automobiles in thick ooze. The Florida Everglades may never be restored. One of our Great Lakes is dying if not already dead. The health of the others is threatened by advancing pollution. Some people regard the Mississippi River as a huge sewage system being filled with untreated excreta and chemicals.

Man extracts nature's subsidy when he fails to develop fully the economy, technology, and political measures. Man must develop the equipment of finance, scientific know-how, and governmental means to break down, dismantle, or reduce the wastes of his communities, agriculture, and industry in a comprehensive manner or suffer infections from the wastes that will invade and surround his physical existence.

Our economy is only partially developed. The costs of raw material, production, transportation, product design, fabrication, distribution, advertising, and sales are included in the cost of our consumer goods. But the leftovers, the wastes—these generally are not paid for. The costs of breaking down or reducing most wastes and byproducts are not prepaid in the market price. Waste materials are simply discarded as garbage. How can nature absorb the thousands of tons of conglomerate garbage? Are bulldozing garbage into lowlands and wetlands, incinerating it, forcing solid wastes into the air, or grinding it into our sewers the only alternatives we will pay for?

112

Our technology is only partially developed. There yet seem to be no biodegradable beer cans or pop bottles — the scourge of parks and roadsides. Ivan Sanderson has observed that even the ubiquitous tissue paper appears to be "almost indestructible." Many demands are made for rapid development of nuclear power, and the federal government appropriates huge sums for it. When it comes to securing money to develop technologies for breaking down radioactive waste, we are slow to perform. The present means of disposing of radioactive waste is to store it underground or in out-of-the-way places or to dilute it. Some experts say dilution is not a safe alternative. Dilution itself eats up nature's limited subsidy. Chemical plants, factories, cattle feedlots, and mines have only partially developed or adopted waste-reducing technologies.

Our political measures are only partially developed. In 1966 Chicago newspapers publicized federal antipollution measures only to have them followed by the dumping of tons of dredged sludge into Lake Michigan by a unit of the federal government. At the Homestead Centennial Symposium at the University of Nebraska, June 11 – 14, 1962, Congressman Wayne N. Aspinall of Colorado outlined the problem of the "fragmentation of legislative responsibility for development of land use policy." Water legislation, too, has grown through a piecemeal approach. Few states have comprehensive, up-to-date natural resource laws. Wisconsin adopted new water resource legislation, effective Aug. 1, 1966. It covers nearly all aspects of water use and misuse. One of the main features is the integration of all water management agencies into a single department of state government. Wisconsin's legislation exemplifies the direction that national, state, and local governments must take to bring political measures into line with present and future needs.

The Christian's encounter with the consequences of civilization on the created world brings forth an echo of Genesis—the Creator wills that man tend His creation.

Tending God's creation today implies that the Christian think and perform as a responsible citizen. At the State of Society Conference for the Northern Great Plains in November 1964, E. W. Mueller said: "Man must examine critically his stewardship of the natural resources to discern whether his management of them is such that they are being developed and used for the enrichment of mankind."

Tending God's creation today implies that the Christian as a responsible citizen will help to develop economic, technological, and political means needed to do the job. This is the public role of the Christian in the stewardship of nature. To do this, he needs to become reasonably informed about governmental and private developments at national, state, and local levels. Too often we tend to confine our acquaintance and interest to either public or private affairs or at one level or the other. The Christian has a responsibility to help make, in ways appropriate to his circumstances, state and national legislation as good as possible through informed participation.

It is important that the institutional church listen to people who are tending God's creation. During a "rural interest" discussion group of a church jurisdictional workshop in 1965 on "social ministry," each of 15 persons was asked to tell of his or her concerns for "rural" areas. A medical doctor spoke of his interest in youth and of his relationship to a boy as a "Big Brother." A housewife talked about helping to develop economic opportunity as one of the bases for family and community life. A farmer related his experience of trying to save a creek from pollution through his participation as a director of a soil and water conservation district. Each contributed something.

The discussion leader helped to identify the significance of what they were doing in terms of Biblical faith. By common consent the meeting was "refreshing and worthwhile."

After the meeting was over, the farmer spoke with the discussion leader. "In 17 years this is the first time a church group has ever listened to anyone telling about soil and water conservation. It may have happened before," he said, "but not in my experience. Many times I've worried that as a Christian maybe I was doing the wrong thing. Now I think that soil and water conservation work is a part of — as was said — 'my ministry.'"

Whatever occupations and avocations Christians may have, they have a responsibility to help care for land and water resources of the nation. Through wise management of the natural resources in their personal care and by participating in agencies for the public stewardship of the earth, Christians can perform a ministry essential for the well-being of our total society — both our metropolitan and our town and country populations.

QUESTIONS FOR DISCUSSION

1. What is meant by the term "town and country" as used by denominations and the U. S. Department of Agriculture? In what ways may the terms "urban" and "rural" be obsolete?

2. What is the difference between the farm population and the rural population? What sector of the rural population is growing most rapidly? What is meant by town and country population?

3. What are state economic areas as defined by Donald J. Bogue and Calvin L. Beale? What is the significance of state economic areas for congregations? What might be the significance of economic subregions and economic regions for statewide or multistate church jurisdictional units? Of economic provinces for denominations?

4. How can continuing education at land-grant universities help congregations and denominations minister to people of our society who live in town and country areas?

5. What are some reasons why the demand for qualified people in agriculture and agribusiness exceeds the supply? What can be done to help youth discover the opportunities in agriculture and agribusiness? How are agricultural exports contributing to the narrowing of the U. S. balance-of-payments gap?

6. Is the "farm income problem" real or imagined? What is the city man's stake in an adequate income for farmers and ranchers? For the town and country

population? Should church people concern themselves with such questions? Why?

7. What is community development according to William and Loureide Biddle? Why are building projects not to be equated with community development?

8. How does the Word of God enter into the process of community development? What is the role of worship in community development? of the pastor? of the layman?

9. What is human relations? In what ways are congregations and communities in town and country areas helping or hindering human relations?

10. What are some constructive actions in human relations that laymen and pastors are taking in town and country areas? What actions may be developed in your area? What does the Gospel offer that is constructive and renewing for human relations?

11. What are some factors in nature that minister to the human spirit? What are the kinds of outdoor recreation facilities in your area according to the seven classes proposed by the Outdoor Recreation Resources Review Commission? What does this say to the ministry of the congregation to which you belong (that is, to the members and pastor)?

12. How is the Christian view of nature different from pantheism? How does the church—the people of God—communicate Biblical values regarding Creation?

13. Why do soil scientists state that the central tenet of land management is use according to capability? What aspect of our land resource is relatively con-

stant and renewable? Partially renewable? Nonrenewable? What are the classes of land in the United States, and what is the significance of the overall classification?

14. What is a watershed? What is the significance of a watershed for controlling erosion, floods, and sedimentation? Why should houses and other permanent buildings not be built on a natural floodplain? How are we polluting both surface and ground water?

15. How are the populations of metropolitan and town and country areas related? How are congregations of metropolitan and town and country areas related?

NOTES

1. *Beauty for America: Proceedings of the White House Conference on Natural Beauty* (Washington, D. C.: U. S. Government Printing Office, 1965), p. 302.

2. *A Place to Live: The Yearbook of Agriculture 1963*, ed. Alfred Stefferud (Washington, D. C. : U. S. Government Printing Office, 1963), p. 533.

3. "Farm Population—Estimates for 1965," U. S. Department of Agriculture, Economic Research Service, Washington, D. C.

4. Donald J. Bogue and Calvin L. Beale, *Economic Areas of the United States* (New York: The Free Press of Glencoe, 1961), p. xl.

5. Ibid., p. xli.

6. Helmut Thielicke, *Man in God's World* (New York: Harper & Row, Publishers, 1963), pp. 31—32.

7. Helmut Thielicke, *Our Heavenly Father* (New York: Harper & Brothers, 1960), pp. 78—79.

8. "Background on U. S. Agriculture," U. S. Department of Agriculture, Office of Information, Leaflet No. 491, revised June 1965, Washington, D. C.

9. *After a Hundred Years: The Yearbook of Agriculture 1962*, ed. Alfred Stefferud (Washington, D. C.: U. S. Government Printing Office, 1962), p. 21.

10. William W. Biddle and Loureide J. Biddle, *The Community Development Process* (New York: Holt, Rinehart & Winston, 1965), p. 78.

11. Lesslie Newbigin, *Trinitarian Faith and Today's Mission* (Richmond, Va.: John Knox Press, 1963), Preface.

12. "Rural Vacation Summer Program," Lutheran Human Relations Association of America, Valparaiso University, Valparaiso, Ind. 46383.

13. *Making the Most of Human Resources Through Rural Community Development: Proceedings of the Thirty-Eighth Conference of the American Country Life Association, Inc.* (Chicago: American Country Life Association, Inc., 1959), pp. 5—7.

14. "The Word in Mississippi" (editorial), Chicago *Sun-Times,* Sept. 22, 1966, p. 51.

15. Thielicke, *Man in God's World,* pp. 72—73.

16. *Land Use Policy and Problems in the United States,* ed. Howard W. Ottoson, (Lincoln: University of Nebraska Press, 1963), pp. 225—27.

17. C. L. McGuinness, *The Role of Ground Water in the National Water Situation* (Washington, D. C.: U. S. Government Printing Office, 1963), pp. 21—23.

FOR FURTHER READING

Breimyer, Harold F. *Individual Freedom and the Economic Organization of Agriculture.* Urbana: University of Illinois Press, 1965.

Environmental Improvement: Air, Water, and Soil, ed. Ralph W. Marquis. Washington, D. C.: The Graduate School, U. S. Department of Agriculture, 1966.

Higbee, Edward. *The Squeeze: Cities Without Space.* New York: William Morrow & Co., 1960.

Iowa State University Center for Agricultural and Economic Development. *Farm Goals in Conflict.* Ames: Iowa State University Press, 1963.

Lord, Russell. *The Care of the Earth: A History of Husbandry.* New York: Thomas Nelson & Sons, 1962.

Mission in the American Outdoors: Concerns of the Church in Leisure-Recreation, ed. E. W. Mueller and Giles C. Ekola. St. Louis: Concordia Publishing House, 1966.

New Thousands in Town and Country. Chicago: National Lutheran Council, Division of American Missions, 1962.

The Silent Struggle for Mid-America: The Church in Town and Country Today, ed. E. W. Mueller and Giles C. Ekola. Minneapolis: Augsburg Publishing House, 1963.

Wright, Jim. *The Coming Water Famine.* New York: Coward-McCann, Inc., 1966.

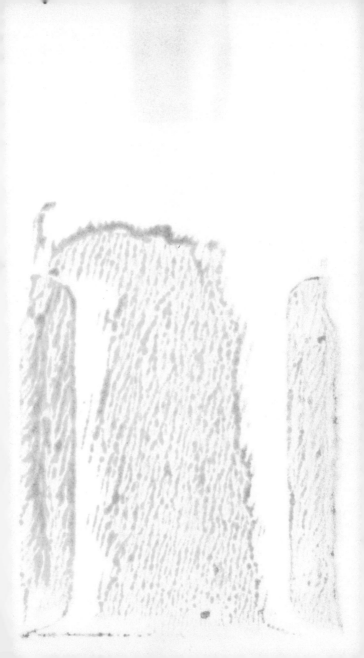

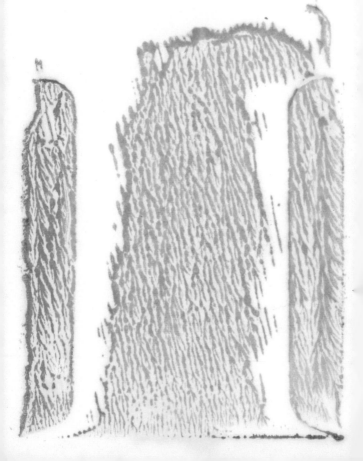